Shrimpy

Shrimpy

A record round-the-world voyage
in an 18 foot yacht

Shane Acton

 PSL Patrick Stephens, Cambridge

Dedication
This book I dedicate to the two great loves of my life:
Super Shrimp—a special boat
and
Iris Derungs—a very special crew.

Also to the many hundreds of friends that we have made throughout
the voyage who, with their kindness, interest, help and generosity
have made this adventure not only possible but beautiful.

And for their undemanding aid I thank: International Yacht Paints,
Rolex Watches and the Cambridge Evening News

First published January 1981

British Library Cataloguing in Publication Data
Acton, Shane
Shrimpy
1. Super Shrimp *(Ship)*
2. Voyages around the world—1951-
I. Title
910'.41   G440.S9/

ISBN 0-85059-524-X

Photoset in 11 on 12 pt Plantin by Manuset Limited, Baldock, Herts.
Printed in Great Britain on City Antique Wove Cream Vol 18 80 gsm,
and bound, by The Garden City Press, Letchworth, Herts, for the
publishers, Patrick Stephens Limited, Bar Hill, Cambridge,
CB3 8EL, England.

Contents

Preamble 6

Analysis of Super Shrimp's achievement 7

Introduction 11

1 Small beginnings, *August 19 1972–June 3 1973* 15

2 Initiation, *June 3–November 23 1973* 20

3 To cross an ocean, *November 23 1973–January 3 1974* 31

4 In steel band lands, *January 3–July 1 1974* 37

5 An Iris blooms in Panama, *July 1–August 15 1974* 44

6 The South American way, *August 15–December 24 1974* 54

7 The Galapagos Islands and the Pacific crossing, *December 24 1974–February 18 1975* 61

8 Nuku Hiva and Tahiti, *February 18–October 23 1975* 75

9 Captain in the Cooks, *October 23 1975–April 15 1976* 82

10 Small dots in the deep, *April 15–July 31 1976* 89

11 Up a river, *July 31–October 6 1976* 93

12 Brisbane the bountiful, *October 6 1976–April 20 1977* 99

13 Behind the Barrier Reef, *April 20–September 17 1977* 105

14 Gove, *September 17 1977–June 10 1978* 112

15 Indonesia—land of islands, *June 10–August 11 1978* 126

16 Single-handed again, *August 11 1978–January 3 1979* 133

17 Across the Indian Ocean, *January 3–March 25 1979* 142

18 Batterings in the Red Sea, *March 25–May 15 1979* 153

19 Shipwrecked, *May 15–July 14 1979* 161

20 Tourist-tarnished Greece, *July 14–August 1 1979* 170

21 The first and final winter, *August 1 1979–June 28 1980* 176

22 The return, *June 28–August 7 1980* 181

Appendices 184

Preamble

The fact that my yacht *Super Shrimp* has become—as far as I know—the smallest boat ever to circumnavigate the globe was not even a consideration when I left England so many years ago. I was not out to beat any records or do any daring deeds, but just to enjoy a rather adventurous way of life. The fact that I had no set plans or timetable was probably the main reason why I was able to complete the circumnavigation—having seen, in the course of my voyage, so many yachts come to grief by trying to stick to a set route and a set date.

The small size of *Super Shrimp* was dictated solely by my limited amount of funds and my impatience to 'get out of the rut'. Having no idea of sailing, in fact, never even having set foot on a yacht before, I feel my choice of craft was very fortunate; I chose her by looking for what I thought was a strong and attractive shape. With my present knowledge, I feel I can say that the 'Caprice', though not so roomy as many of her competitors, nor as hairy to sail, has a design a cut above the rest. This, coupled with the fact that her builder was much more than just a mere carpenter, easily made up for her lack of size.

In the following account of the voyage, I am aware that there are many drastic changes of style and opinions, perhaps even outright contradictions. This is because the writing has been spaced out over the eight years of the voyage and, though sorely tempted to change many things, I have decided to let them stand—to give a truer account of my interpretation of events at the time they happened.

S.J. ACTON
Histon, Cambridge,
September 1980.

Analysis of Super Shrimp's achievement

D.H. Clarke, writer for the *Guinness Book of Records*

These days superlatives concerning the sport of sailing yachts across oceans seem to the casual observer to come into the category of 'ten a penny'. So in order to understand exactly Shane Acton's achievement in *Super Shrimp* it is necessary to go back to the early days of endeavour in small vessels.

This sport, pastime—call it what you will—can be described thus: 'The process of taking any type of boat or vessel, regardless of size, on a voyage beyond the continental shelf of the country where the voyage commences, by a person or persons not engaged in any form of maritime livelihood—excluding the yacht trade or any part thereof—shall be regarded as participation in the Blue Water Game.'

Accepting this definition as it stands, the Blue Water Game (BWG) began in the middle of the 19th century, particularly in the case of small vessels. Now the problem that these craft set in those early days was the very simple one that nobody bothered to define the difference between large and small. Until recent years, any yacht that seemed to a landlubber to be impossibly limited for the task in hand was described as a 'small boat' (although the word 'boat' is wrong, since it correctly refers only to open craft, propelled by paddles or oars). Since the Atlantic has been crossed by yachts, sailed single-handed, as large as 236 ft (71.92 m) length overall (LOA), and as small as 5 ft $11\frac{7}{8}$ in (1.8256 m) LOA, it follows that a positive division between the sizes has been long overdue.

Listing all the participants in the BWG from the beginning (around 1850) to 1899, revealed a total of 65 attempts in craft ranging from 9 ft (2.74 m) LOA to just under 50 ft (15.24 m) LOA, with slightly more in the larger category beginning at just over 54 ft (16.46 m) and rising into the giant sizes. A division between 'small' and 'large' therefore became obvious. Of the 'small' category, some 30 were *very* small—up to 21 ft (6.40 m) LOA—and so a further division was apparent; the same ruling applied to larger sizes. The only necessity after this discovery was to translate the figures into the nearest round metric equivalent, with the following result:

Nomenclature for LOA size division of craft used in the BWG

Small	Midget size:	up to 6.50 m (21 ft 4 in) LOA
	Medium size:	from 6.51 m to 15.50 m (50 ft 10in) LOA
Large	Major size:	from 15.51 m to 24.50 m (80 ft 5 in) LOA
	Giant size:	over 24.50 m (80 ft 5 in) LOA

In competitive terms, therefore, *Super Shrimp* comes into the midget size of yacht, and comparisons should only be made in this category. The first midget to cross the Atlantic measured 20 ft × 6 ft 6 in (6.10 × 1.98 m). Named *City of Ragusa*, in 1870 she was sailed from Liverpool to Cork to Boston in 98 days (84 from Cork) by Austrian-born, British-nationalised Pietro Di Costa and Irishman John C. Buckley. In 1871 she sailed from New York to Queenstown in 40 days, captained by Englishman E.R.W. Hayter with another Austrian, Nicholas Primoraz, as crew. In 1883, Bernard Gilboy, an American born of Irish immigrant parents, crossed the Pacific alone and nonstop, from San Francisco to Queensland, Australia, in his 18 ft × 6 ft (5.50 × 1.83 m) schooner-rigged *Pacific*, taking 162 days. And it is credited (though as yet unsubstantiated) that a Captain Cleveland of Salem, USA, sailed a 15 ft (4.57 m) sloop across the Indian and Pacific oceans, from Cape Town to Alaska in 1800-1; another possible voyage along a similar route, but again unsubstantiated, was made by two Norwegians in a 16 ft (4.88 m) folding sail boat, from Liverpool to Rio de Janeiro to Perth, Australia, in 1879, taking 330 days, including stops.

Since those days many voyages across the oceans of the world have been successfully completed in midget yachts, though none achieved a circumnavigation until 1955-59, when Englishman John Guzzwell sailed single-handed round the world, westabout via the Panama Canal, in his home-built Bermudan yawl *Trekka*, 20 ft 10 in × 6 ft 6 in × 4 ft 6 in (6.35 × 1.98 × 1.37 m). Of the 70 or so singlehanders who have achieved this feat since the first—the celebrated Joshua Slocum, in 1895-8—only one other has gone round in a midget yacht. He was Japanese, Hiroshi Aoki, who in 1971-4 went eastabout via Cape Horn in his home-built Bermudan yawl, *Ahodori II*, which was fractionally smaller than *Trekka*, measuring 20 ft 8 in × 6 ft 7 in × 4 ft 3 in (6.31 × 2.00 × 1.30 m). These craft were sailed single-handed, yet it will be seen that they were over two feet longer than *Super Shrimp*, which at times carried two people aboard.

Needless to say, when stores and water for two are carried normally the size of the yacht, through necessity, has to be larger. As a result, two-crew circumnavigations have been made in much larger craft (compared with *Super Shrimp*). The smallest of these were: Rollo Gebhard (Germany), 24 ft 4 in (7.40 m) LOA, *Solveig III*, 1967-70, east-west via the Panama Canal, with an occasional crew, but mostly single-

8

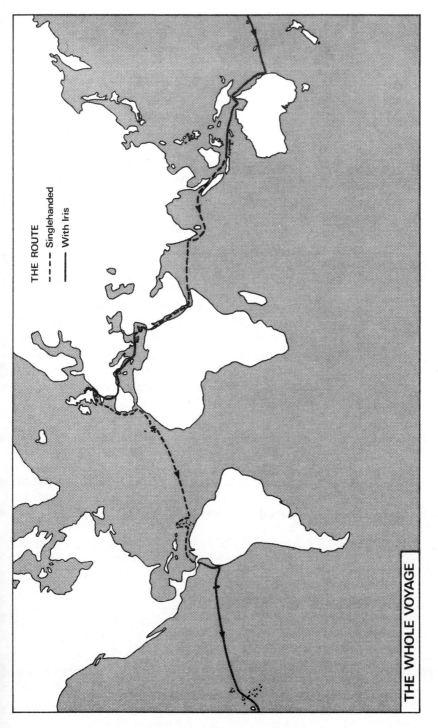

THE ROUTE
- - - - Singlehanded
———— With Iris

THE WHOLE VOYAGE

handed; Alain Raymond (France), 24 ft (7.31 m) LOA, *Exocet*, 1974-6, east-west via the Panama Canal, with one crew; Ian Mitchel and his wife Jan, (New Zealand), 25 ft (7.62 m), *Caprice*, 1974-77, also east-west via the Panama Canal.

So from all these circumnavigations, *Super Shrimp* was the third midget yacht to sail round the world, the smallest to do so, and certainly the smallest to take a crew for part of the way.

These remarkable superlatives are not quite all that Shane and Iris achieved. It is likely that together during the Pacific crossing they were the smallest two-crew vessel trans-Pacific east-west, and it is also possible that Shane, singlehanded during the crossing of the Indian Ocean, sailed the smallest yacht westwards across this ocean. These possibilities must stand in credit until a positive assessment can be made at a later date, for so many voyages are being made—a large number of which are unpublicised—that it is impossible to be immediately specific about some feats.

These are the simple facts about this circumnavigation in a 'small boat', which may seem to oversimplify all the hardship and hazards that were faced. And I have said nothing about the secondary superlatives, such as finance—or, rather, lack of it—and seamanship and navigational skills, which were equally sparse in the early stages. There are, indeed, records for such matters too, but it would be invidious for me to quote them. That Shane Acton overcame all these, setting forth from Cambridge as a green sailor, and returning eight years later with a sound vessel, in good health, an additional advantage of a crew, and with invaluable experience in sail and adventure that money can never buy, is a record of personal pride that is exclusively his. For although, one day, someone may sail round the world in an even smaller yacht, nobody can possibly take away his memories of his successfully executed voyage. In retrospect, as the years pass, this personal recording of an outstanding feat will always remain as a happiness that is beyond price, and this is the greatest superlative of them all.

Introduction

Damn you Shane Acton! Barnacles to you Shane Acton! I hate you Shane Acton!

It is scarcely possible to open the newspapers these days without being confronted by your damnably happy face and your confoundedly happy words.

So now here I am, sitting in the gathering gloom of a sodden English autumn watching the mortgages go up and the exports go down as I leaf through the Acton scrapbook and try to come to terms with it all.

'We became enveloped in the sheer beauty of the South Seas', wrote Shane Acton from Taiohae in the Marquesas.

'The chief of the nearest village, who turned out to be immensely interesting, invited us to a party that evening', wrote Shane Acton from Fiji.

'One of the biggest things I have discovered is that the human race is much nicer than I thought it was', wrote Shane Acton from, so help me, the Friendly Isles.

'In the clear, calm waters of Academy Bay we watched the fish clean the bottom of *Super Shrimp* and fed the yellow warblers from our hands', wrote Shane Acton from the Galapagos.

Thus he goes on, month after month. And thus I go on, getting gloomier and gloomier.

Forgive me, gentle reader, but I cannot bring myself to quote further examples from the despatches sent to the *Cambridge Evening News** by this young man since he set out down the Cam from Cambridge eight years ago with £20 in his pocket and the sublimely simple intention of sailing round the world in *Super Shrimp*, an 18-foot sailing boat of the sort used by weekend splashers-about. Forgive me if I push the scrapbook aside. It is too painful. Too distressing. Suffice it to say, that if you have not been following the singularly successful saga of Shane and *Super Shrimp* then do not, I beseech you, do not start now. Do not read this book. It is dangerous. It will bring you nothing but the misery

* Throughout his voyage Shane sent regular despatches to his local newspaper, of which Christopher South is Assistant Editor (News).

suffered by those of us already hooked on this exasperating wanderer's picture of paradise. And should you glimpse one day from the corner of an idling eye what seems to be a newspaper article by Shane Acton, then I beg you to rip it out of the paper. Rip out the whole page and hurl it in the fire. Do not risk giving it to your hamsters as bedding. Do not attempt to recycle the page by adding it to the compost heap. Just burn it, lest some potent fragment of Acton prose may survive to hook you in an unguarded moment. Imagine what would happen if you were cleaning out the hamsters and noticed a shred of paper bearing, for example, the words: 'When we were high enough to find a cool breeze we would sit and gaze at the sea while eating a freshly picked mango or paw paw, or perhaps drinking the cool refreshing milk of a young, green coconut'. I know full well what would happen to me under such circumstances. I would scrabble around, wrecking the hamsters' nest in a feverish search for the other paradisal pieces of paper. I would find a scrap saying: 'Although perpetually broke, I always eat well, sleep well and find new adventure every day,' and by then I would be totally hooked and totally miserable. Why miserable? In one word: Envy. I am consumed, eaten up, tormented, tortured and twisted with envy for Shane Acton. He does all the things I would like to do and now, not satisfied even with taking aboard his boat a beautiful blonde called Iris, not satisfied with navigating completely round the world using a plastic sextant, not satisfied with any of these achievements, he is now even becoming world famous. This profoundly irritating young man is breaking world records. Meanwhile, the only world records I am likely to break are for sitting on my backside and going green with envy. I wish to heaven I had never heard of Shane Acton. I wish a tweeny-weeny tidal wave would hit him—just big enough to sweep away his pencil so he could not write any more. I wish I could believe he is henpecked by Iris. That would do me so much good. I would feel quite content with my lot and quite resigned to my own inadequacies if I thought Shane Acton was nagged by his pretty Swiss miss.

But there seems little hope of any such comfort. The damn man is unsinkably successful, unbearably buoyant.

Damn you, Shane Acton! Barnacles to you, Shane Acton!

Christopher South

CAPRICE

designed by Robert Tucker

Although the hard-chine hull has a fine entry, the forebody is deep and buoyant. With its generous beam and freeboard, the Caprice should be a dry boat in a seaway.

Three-eighth inch marine plywood is used for the construction of the hull and for the decking, which is well cambered and supported on oak beams. The twin keels of oak, ballasted with lead or iron, are through-bolted to the hull which is stiffened in way of the keels with wooden supports and steel strapping.

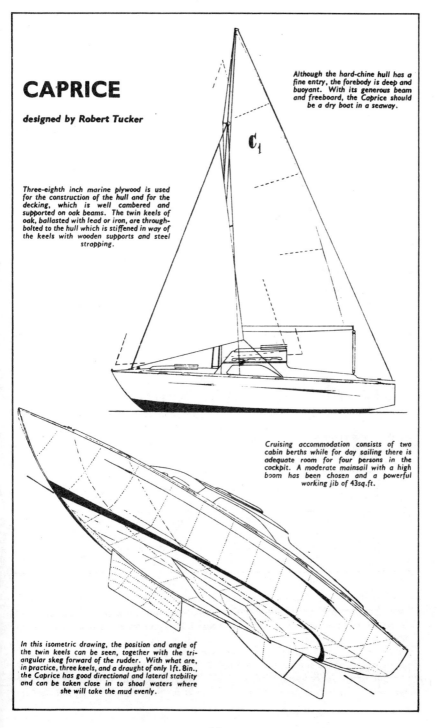

Cruising accommodation consists of two cabin berths while for day sailing there is adequate room for four persons in the cockpit. A moderate mainsail with a high boom has been chosen and a powerful working jib of 43sq.ft.

In this isometric drawing, the position and angle of the twin keels can be seen, together with the triangular skeg forward of the rudder. With what are, in practice, three keels, and a draught of only 1ft. 8in., the Caprice has good directional and lateral stability and can be taken close in to shoal waters where she will take the mud evenly.

13

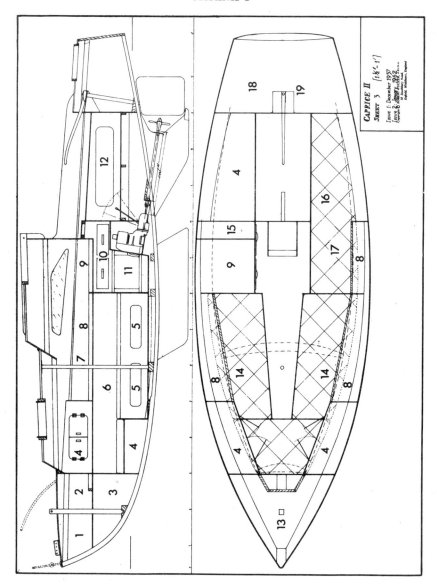

This vessel, which is a 'Caprice' Class II, is very similar to Shrimpy but has some extra refinements. Shrimpy had no built-in engine, no mast support tube and the front portion of the superstructure was flush with the deck (see page 13). The Caprice was designed by Robert Tucker.

Key: 1 Forepeak. **2** 2″ × 2″ Kingpost. **3** Chain locker. **4** Locker. **5** Access holes. **6** 3″-4″ Berth cushions. **7** Mast support tube. **8** Shelf. **9** Galley. **10** Drawers. **11** Sliding doors. **12** Watertight hatch. **13** Forepeak shelf. **14** Berth. **15** Compass well. **16** Quarter berth. **17** Hinged chart table may be fitted over head of quarter berth. **18** Lazarette. **19** Rudder-head frame.

1

Small beginnings
August 19 1972–June 3 1973

The city of Cambridge is 60 miles from the sea but it does have a river, and it was here at the age of 12 that I launched my very first boat, a secondhand canvas canoe bought as a birthday present by my parents. I had endless hours of fun from this old canoe and, by the time I left school to join the Royal Marines, it had more patches than canvas, but it had instilled in me a love of boats that has remained ever since.

After I had finished my basic training with the Marines, I chose to enter their Landing Craft Section which involved being taught the handling of small craft as well as having duty on ships that visited such idyllic places as the Seychelle Islands. Then for a while I turned my back on the sea and roamed around America for a year and then to Europe for a time, but always returned to Cambridge penniless—having run out of visas, work permits and other red tape requirements. It was then that the idea struck me—if I had a boat and no visa I could just sail along to the next country! From there the idea blossomed, aided by the growing public interest in the doings of small boats, into the realisation that a little ship on the big sea was what I really wanted from life.

Now that I had a goal to aim for, I went to work with a will (well almost), at yet another unskilled, uninteresting but fund-providing job. During this time I read all I could get hold of in the way of books about small boats. After about six months of saving I decided it was time for a short rest, so I bought a fibreglass canoe and put it and myself on a train to Llangollen, Wales, and spent a glorious week canoeing back to Cambridge through the rivers and canals of England. Now I was getting impatient with my savings and rather fed up with work—I had been hard at it for at least eight months—so with what money I had saved I bought a small inland motor cruiser—with visions of touring the canals of England and Europe. But this, however, was a compromise and deep down I knew it. Luckily I was able to sell the cruiser for a profit a few months later and then, with £500 in my pocket, I started looking for a yacht.

If you want to buy a good seaworthy secondhand yacht, Cambridge is not the best place to do it, so I had to spend precious amounts of hard-gained money looking around. Eventually I found her, and it was love

15

at first sight in a garage on Hayling Island. She was a 'Caprice' Class bilge keel Mark I built in marine ply by C.E. Clark Limited and, although ten years old, had been kept in superb condition by her owner—she cost every penny I possessed!

I had my boat now but no money and winter was on its way, so I had her transported to Cambridge, moored her on the river and moved on board. It was back to work once more, but I could now spend the money as I earned it on essential equipment for my little boat and life was good.

At the time she was called *Wee D'orch*. 'Well, that will have to go', I thought, no matter how much ill luck mariners attach to the changing of a ship's name, and so I registered her at London as *Super Shrimp*—but, of course, she is just plain 'Shrimpy' to her friends.

Time was flying by now and I was beginning to learn the truth of the saying that a ship is never 100 per cent ready for sea. So on August 19 1972 I reckoned we were as near ready as we would ever be for sea trials, which was to consist of a passage from the Wash to Falmouth, calling at anywhere that took my fancy on the way.

It was time for the black sheep to say goodbye to his family once again. My parents would much rather I was in a job with 'prospects', living in a nice mortgaged house with a wife, 2.3 kids and 1.6 cars, but I'm afraid that's not for me!

The first entry in the first logbook for Shrimpy reads: 'SAT 19th August 1100 hours—left moorings at Cambridge. Course: down river'. We were off!

The next morning we passed through Denver Lock into the tidal waters of the Wash and I was sure I could hear Shrimpy give a sigh of relief as she touched salt water again. At the port of King's Lynn which is in the mouth of this river, I could erect the mast—having passed my last bridge for many a year.

It took me quite a while to figure out where all the wires and ropes went, for never before had I set foot on a yacht (let alone sailed one). Eventually, everything seemed to be in its right place and I was ready to attempt my first sail.

The next port of call was Wells-next-the-Sea where, using the tides, I got two brand new coats of antifouling on before horrible things could start chomping their way into my little boat. Then off we went down the Channel learning all we could about each other and stopping each night in a small port or a sheltered anchorage because I dared not yet try to sail in darkness. After only one bad incident where we had to limp into Cowes with a broken tiller, we reached Falmouth safe and sound and penniless on Friday, September 22. My thoughts as I tied up to the Town Quay at Falmouth were firstly, to find a mooring for the winter and, secondly, to find a job (yet again) until the warm weather returned.

I reported my arrival to the Harbour Master and asked if there were any moorings available for the winter. He thought this a great joke and told me they were booked solid for about five years, but I could use the visitors buoy for £1 a day or anchor in the open roads for nothing. When I asked him about the possibility of finding a job for the winter season in Falmouth he expressed great doubt and I think he also doubted my sanity. He was, however, very helpful and suggested I contact the Penryn Harbour Master about the possibility of a mud berth further up river. At this point we were interrupted by noisy shouting and horn blowing—to discover that I had left Shrimpy tied to the steps the local ferry used and it had just arrived full of workers anxious to get home. I hurriedly jumped aboard and put Shrimpy to anchor for the night.

The next morning I set off on foot (I couldn't afford the bus fare) to Penryn. It is about three or four miles up river from Falmouth and at low tide there is not a drop of water to be seen! It was low tide when I reached the quay and I discovered that the Harbour Master was only available at high tide, so I sat in a caravan-cum-cafe on Penryn Quay to await his arrival. It was here that I met Roger (who was to become a great friend) and, while chatting, I told him of my predicament.

'Well', he said, 'Sailors' Creek is the place for you. It will cost nothing, and there are half a dozen of us living on boats there who will look after you. I'll point out where it is from the quay here and I'll be down this afternoon to make sure you're OK.'

The 'Acton luck' had struck again (one of these days I'll land on my head instead of my feet and wonder what's hit me). Needless to say, I took his advice and sailed Shrimpy into Sailors' Creek that afternoon, and there we stayed until I left England. It was, and I hope still is, the ideal spot for a yacht which can take the ground (when I left the powers-that-be were trying to get permission to put a concrete and plastic marina there). The creek is protected from all winds and the tide comes in with the docility of bath water; the ground is flat and hard right up to the shore (my bow line was tied to a tree); there is a stream at the head of the creek providing good fresh water and the place is far enough away from civilisation to be secluded, yet near enough to commute to work—via the small village of Flushing a mile away and a ten-minute ferry ride to Falmouth.

Roger, as good as his word, arrived later in the afternoon and introduced me to the rest of the residents of the Creek; the main ones being Frank Lang and Jerry Brown. To say Jerry knew a lot about sailing was putting it mildly, and Frank, while being very knowledgeable about boats, knew everyone worth knowing in Falmouth—and everyone worth knowing knew Frank.

During the months that I stayed in the Creek I was to find that these

17

three people, Frank, Roger and Jerry, were the most generous, most helpful and most interesting I had ever known. An example of this occurred almost immediately I arrived. We were all on Frank's boat *Pride of the West*, getting acquainted, when I happened to mention that I needed a job. The very next day there was a knock on my boat and there was Mike—one of Frank's numerous friends—who said: 'You start work Monday'.

Mike (and Graham who I met later) owned a small building firm and were 'working directors', as Mike termed it, and the whole outfit was locally known as 'Python's Circus'. Although I was only employed as a labourer I found that here was, for the first time, a job I could really enjoy. This was because the firm was so small that I was allowed to try my hand at many aspects of the trade and the sites were in such awkward places on uneven ground that many ingenious ideas had to be thought up in order to cope. My ideas, as those of the other labourers, were listened to by the 'working directors' and all the while the end product of our labours was visible for all to see. All this, in an atmosphere of good humour and with great workmates, made for halcyon days during my stay at Falmouth.

*   *   *

In preparing Shrimpy for sea I made no structural changes at all for she seemed to me to be adequately strong enough, although the large cockpit which did not self-drain was worrying (but I didn't change it until I reached the Cook Islands!). She was a three-berth design, but as I only needed one berth the quarter berth was converted to water storage and the starboard berth into a chart table with storage underneath. The bow and stern and various other small spaces were packed with polystyrene foam for buoyancy. I had a running sail made up by Penrose, the local sail maker, to my own design. This consisted of a diamond shape, hanked up the middle on a two-inch ridge that stood proud, and was set by means of a galvanised tube lashed athwartships, and two sheets leading through blocks to the tiller. With this arrangement, plus a couple of resistor sheets on the tiller, I found that, after a bit of practice, I could get Shrimpy to self-steer on any course on which running sails are feasible.

I thought I would have problems when it came to storing all my gear plus food and water (calculated for 60 days) but I found that I had plenty of room. Water, 30 gallons, was stored in one-gallon plastic containers in the port quarter berth and starboard cockpit locker. My argument was that in using one-gallon cans I could keep the boat trimmed more easily and that the empty cans would act as buoyancy. Paraffin, five gallons, was also stored in the starboard locker. Tinned food, 120 tins approximately, went under the port and starboard berths. Dry food all went in the galley locker. Vegetables went under the berths forward. Various items that needed to be kept completely dry went into 20 square Tupperware containers which stacked in rows under the chart table.

The table and various other small compartments I made with varnished hardboard, which looks just as good as wood but is much lighter—there is also a considerable money factor!

Cooking was done on a primus stove (which was eventually put in gimbals at Las Palmas). It is more tedious to light than gas but so much safer. In harbour I use a small chemical toilet but at sea this is impractical (have you ever tried?) and there is running water all around the boat anyway.

A safety harness was permanently attached to the boat and to me 24 hours a day, and I would suggest that anyone in a boat so small and sailing alone is an idiot not to do this.

While all this preparation was underway, many people took an interest and would pop in now and then, but much time was spent with Frank, Jerry, Roger and their many friends. One day a small dinghy was rowed into the creek by a Swiss guy called Henri. He had sailed from Norway in his converted fishing boat *Havglimpt* with a friend called Heini, and was on his way to Las Palmas. Neither of them knew any celestial navigation and he asked me to teach him, but the next day I discovered that they had left. I was quite worried—but without cause as you will see later.

By April, work was finished on the boat and I had enough money to buy stores, with a bit to spare. So I took some time out to go back to Cambridge to visit my parents.

On my return to Falmouth I got all the stores and water aboard and now had a definite answer for all those many people who constantly asked, 'When are you going, when are you going?' 'Sunday June 3' I replied now, instead of 'Whenever I'm ready.'

2

Initiation
June 3–November 23 1973

On Sunday morning the sun was shining and the wind was north-west; conditions were ideal. Frank came over in his skiff and offered me a tow down the harbour, which I gratefully accepted. When we were opposite the port entrance I dropped his line and said goodbye, wondering how long it would be until I met such friends again.

After I had cleared land, I set a course for Cape Finisterre with the running sail up and decided to check my celestial navigation (sunsights) while I still knew where I was. I knew all the theory, having been given a birthday present of the book *Rantzen's Little Ship Celestial Navigation* by my sister, but practice was the thing, so I gathered together my plastic sextant, 'Mickey Mouse' wristwatch and Japanese radio and got to work.

Immediately after working out the first position line I knew something was wrong as it put me 600 miles out to sea. After some thought I was forced to the conclusion that BST is not GMT and tried again. This was more like it; the three sights crossed exactly and gave me a perfect position. It is rare to get an absolute position, especially on your very first attempt, but this was due, in part, to the scale of the chart I was using, for when I bought my charts my head was in the clouds and, although I had large scale ones of the Pacific, Panama, the West Indies and the Canaries, the only one that showed England also showed South America and a pencil line drawn on it was—according to the scale—about three miles thick!

The reason, I think, that celestial navigation is considered by many to be a mystic art is because so many people have such fascinating and hilarious stories about their first attempts, such as being positioned in the overtaking lane on the M1 or running aground on the Alps. This is only lack of practice, however, and it is really extremely simple. Given someone who can add, subtract and tell the time, I could teach them all they need know for navigating a yacht in one day. This is not boasting, it is just illustrating how simple celestial navigation is.

The next item on the agenda was lunch. I had not yet perfected the art of getting Shrimpy to self-steer under the running sail, so I took the primus stove out into the cockpit and, wedging it between my feet, I managed to get it going and prepared lunch while all the time steering with one hand. What did I have for lunch? Chips, fried eggs, baked beans and pancakes to follow! Well, I though that if I could do that for my first meal there would be no further problems. Pancakes, incidentally, have become a firm favourite of mine at sea, as all the ingredients will keep indefinitely (provided powdered milk is used) and they make a splendid substitute for bread, which I really miss on a long trip.

Things were going well, and the weather was perfect for the first five days. After I had got out of the shipping lanes I was taking all my sails down each night and sleeping for a good ten hours, with a paraffin lamp left to burn merrily in the rigging. On the sixth day it got a bit rough, about force seven, and the seas became very steep, but Shrimpy took it well, bobbing about quite happily and only when I tried to put a small sail up did she threaten to pitch-pole (turn stern over bow).

After ten days I rounded Cape Finisterre and on the twelfth day, with just a breath of wind, I ghosted into the small Portugese port of Viana do Castelo. This is a place seldom visited by yachts; why this should be I fail to understand as the entrance is simple, the mooring is safe and calm—even in hurricane-force winds—all the officials are courteous and efficient and the little town is beautiful.

As I tied up to the quay with my 'Q' flag flying, I was told in a mixture of sign language and schoolboy French—both of which I speak fluently—that the Harbour Master was at lunch and would be arriving in half-an-hour. I decided to have a meal while I waited and, with an audience of fascinated children, proceeded to cook in the cockpit. When the Harbour Master arrived, I gathered my papers together, jumped on to the quay and fell flat on my face—the land was rocking violently and I couldn't stand up, so the Harbour Master sat down and we filled in his forms on the pavement, encircled by a grinning crowd. As soon as we finished the formalities a man from the crowd introduced himself in perfect American-English. He was Henrique Duart, an American fisherman, who owned a large trawler and had come back to visit this town where he had been born and had worked as a fisherman until he emigrated. He still knew many of the locals and had money to burn, so we were very popular as he took me on a tour of the town, which included a visit to his parents and numerous drinks at the bars he remembered. When I returned to the boat I found a big steel yacht had arrived; this was the first example I saw of the many 'Joshua' Class yachts I was to meet on my voyage. The French family on board invited me to a delicious lunch cooked by a delicious girl. After I had said my goodbyes, I went to ask the Harbour Master how much I owed him and, to my pleasant surprise, he said 'Nothing, in Portugal visiting yachts are guests'. I wish this attitude was more widespread in the so-called 'civilised world'.

I set sail at two o'clock and arrived in the next port, Varzim, at six. This is a tiny fishing port with a glorious flat sandy beach at its head. So, much to the concern of the local fishermen, I threw out my kedge anchor and headed straight for the beach. They thought I had grounded accidentally and one of them started pushing the boat off. I smiled, shook my head, jumped off the bow and ran my bower anchor up the beach. They were amazed when the tide went out, leaving Shrimpy standing solidly upright on, not one, but two keels sticking out of her bilges! This trick was to surprise many more small port inhabitants who had never seen bilge keel yachts before. The man who had tried to 'rescue' the boat had sacrificed a dry pair of trousers to do so, so I therefore invited him on board for supper. Although he came on board and took a great interest in Shrimpy, he refused any food saying that it was I who was the guest not he. I did manage to force a cup of coffee on to him, however, and he left after inviting me to lunch with him the next day and also promising to show me around the town.

As I was settling down for the night there came a knock on my boat. It was the local policeman whose job it was to guard the harbour. Although he was still meant to be on duty, he invited me out for a few drinks in an old 'port wine' cellar. A few drinks turned into many and we returned to the harbour just in time for him to be relieved!

The next day, after my promised guided tour and meal, plus two hours televiewing, I left at two o'clock and sailed down the coast to the harbour of Lexioes, arriving there at six. Lexioes is a man-made commercial harbour jutting out from the shore just north of Oporto. It is not very interesting, but there are good moorings for yachts and a local yacht club, and it saves having to sail up the river in order to visit Oporto, for Shrimpy had no engine.

It was here that I met Chris and Sue for the first time, with their very attractive little yacht called *Easybeat*. They invited me aboard for a meal and a chat and, as we talked, it was apparent that they were a bit disenchanted with the sea at that moment. They had spent much time fitting out in England—they said they had overprepared—that's as maybe, but at least they had left, which seems to be the hardest part of any adventure, although it only involves untying two lines or pulling up an anchor. On this, their very first voyage with a yacht, they had been dogged with bad weather, seasickness and general discomfort and, not having seen a smaller vessel on their trip so far, were unhappy about the size of their boat. Well, we can't have fellow travellers in this state can we? So I did my best to convince them that their boat was a palace (well compared to Shrimpy it was) and I advised them to take Avomine tablets at the beginning of each trip, which I do to great effect. They seemed quite startled at some of my practices, such as sleeping during

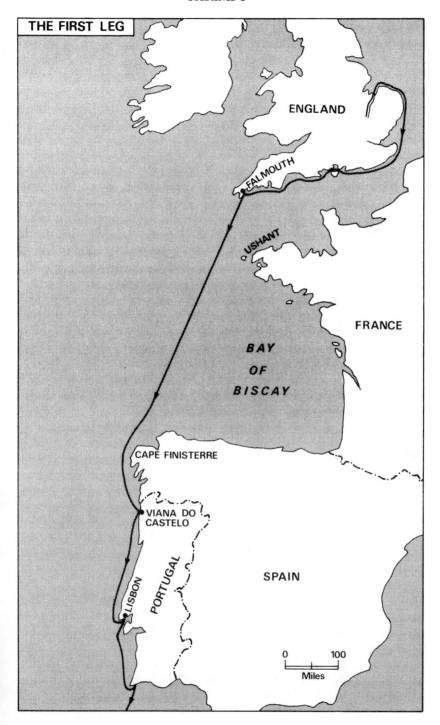

THE FIRST LEG

ENGLAND

FALMOUTH

USHANT

FRANCE

BAY

OF

BISCAY

CAPE FINISTERRE

VIANA DO
CASTELO

PORTUGAL

LISBON

SPAIN

0   100

Miles

the night, just letting the boat drift, and when I told them that on my ungimballed primus, the menu was mainly chips and pancakes, Sue was astounded. I am glad to say that when we met again in Las Palmas the story was quite different and I was told, over an *Easybeat* meal of *chips* and *pancakes* that the weather was good, seasickness had gone and all was well! I like to think (it boosts my ego) that in some small way I helped.

After a short stop in the lagoon and port of Aveiro—of interest only to motorboats—I sailed into the popular holiday resort of Figueiro do Foz but, just as I entered the harbour, a motor launch came screaming towards me, its horns blaring and with much waving and shouting on deck. I was ordered to anchor where I was and not attempt to go any further. So, wondering what on earth I had done to warrant this, I dropped the hook overboard and waited. It turned out that there was to be a powerboat race in the harbour the next day and practice was taking place, so I had to wait until it was over before I could enter the port. Instead of being annoyed at officialdom, I was thankful for a timely warning (as was the case throughout Portugal) and invited the crew aboard for coffee. By the time practice was over, the wind had died, so the launch towed me into port, snuggled Shrimpy into a quiet berth and said goodnight.

The next day I watched the powerboat race which turned out to be quite amusing. They were racing round and round an oval course with a marker buoy at each end, until one of the buoys came adrift and slowly sailed towards the other. Now we were watching about 30 powerboats flying in ever decreasing circles and I was beginning to wonder in which of the 'classic' ways they would disappear but, sadly, the rogue buoy was re-moored before this could happen.

I left with the tide the next morning and sailed straight into a calm. It lasted for two days and I was becoming frustrated. Then, when I ran out of cigarettes, I became downright angry and started swearing at the wind and sea. King Neptune soon took offence at this and sent a force six wind from the exact direction I wished to go, so as I beat into it, getting soaked and cold, I had to spend the rest of the day apologising to him. When I had served my term of punishment I was rewarded by fair winds blowing me into São Martinho do Porto. This is a beautiful natural lagoon of about half a mile radius, almost completely landlocked, and protected from the sea by 500-foot cliffs, with a nice flat sandy beach just made for Shrimpy. There is just one tiny village on the shore and the place is a haven away from the rigours of the sea and the land. A day later I, rather reluctantly, left this lagoon and set sail for Lisbon. The wind was mild and the sea flat so I had the running sail and the main up. The wind gradually increased but as it was dead aft I hung on to the sails and by the time I reached Lisbon bay it was blowing about force six and I was screaming along. Now it so happened that, at that moment, there were about 20 racing yachts bobbing around under the headland trying to get out of Lisbon bay and wondering what wind they would find and which sails they would need. When I hove into sight all they could discern was a little boat with all her sails up, so out came the big lightweight genoas and fairweather sails. When they eventually hit the wind it was quite fun to watch and there was much good natured swearing when I passed them (they were heading up the coast). That evening I entered the crowded yacht basin, nudging my way between thousands of pounds worth of beautiful yachts and settled down for the night.

Lisbon, to my pleasant surprise, turned out to be the most beautiful city I have ever seen and I 'toured' it for four days. It has an intermingling of old and new buildings that all seem to fit; from the great suspension bridge to the ancient markets. The public transport system of buses, suburban trains, tramcars and the underground are all very efficiently run and the whole town is so clean it is unbelievable.

Leaving Lisbon and after a brief stop at Sines, I rounded Cape St Vincent and steered into a small fishing port in its lee called Angrinha. Here I had to make a decision, whether to go into the Mediterranean or to head for Morocco and the Canaries. I decided to ask the gods and, in reply, got a northern wind—Morocco it was.

So, on Saturday July 7, I set out for Casablanca. This is quite a dangerous stretch of water for a small boat as you have to cross all the main shipping lines to and from the Mediterranean, and for four days I was awake most of the time. My navigation, subsequently, suffered and when I reached the latitude of Casablanca I saw that I was ten miles out to sea. As the wind was north I decided to give the place a miss and sail on down the coast to El Yadida. This meant that I would run out of cigarettes again so I was not too happy and when I espied a local fisherman in a rowboat, I hailed him and asked if he could sell me some. He came alongside and offered me just one cigarette—his very last—and asked me for a drink of water in exchange, which I gave him. Then an idea struck him: why don't I anchor Shrimpy and go ashore with him for lunch? Well, I was a bit dubious about this for two reasons. Firstly, there was no really safe anchorage just an open stretch of beach and, secondly, I had not yet 'officially' entered the country, but as his tent (his permanent home) was on the beach and I would be able to keep an eye on Shrimpy, I anchored and jumped into the rowboat.

Once ashore, I was introduced to the rest of the fishermen—about a dozen in all—and after I had convinced them that I had sailed Shrimpy from England (she was smaller than their rowboats) they were very interested and we all sat down to lunch, eaten from a communal bowl in the centre of the table, and lashings of the very sweet mint tea, chatting away amiably in sign language. It was in the midst of this feast that the local police arrived. Some busybody had told them of my visit, apparently with the hope of a reward. There were two of them, the Captain of the village of Bir Jdid and one of his Lieutenants, and very smart they looked too in their perfectly pressed uniforms. When I explained that I was just a tourist on his way from England to anywhere, I was given a long hard stare and was asked to let them search my boat. I agreed with a smile and we all piled into a small fibreglass dinghy one of the fishermen owned. Now I'm afraid the sea was a bit too rough for this little dinghy and we all got absolutely soaked and the Lieutenant was badly seasick in the 100 yards trip out to Shrimpy, so the search was quick and I was asked to bring my papers back ashore for, as the Captain explained: 'The situation seems a bit unusual and I'm afraid I must check your papers'. Well, I had to agree that it was, so off we went to Bir Jdid police station about ten miles away (after the Captain had warned the fishermen of what would happen to them if anything happened to Shrimpy). Although the police were very courteous and good-humoured—even to the extent of drafting an English-speaking Lieutenant from a nearby village to take me out for a meal—it took 26 hours to get my papers checked. Eventually I was driven back to the beach and, by this time, I was very anxious about Shrimpy, but I needn't have worried as there she was bobbing away quite happily. My fishermen friends had been really put out by this incident and, despite my assertions that I had enjoyed the adventure, were continually apologising as they led me towards a meal that had obviously been cooked and kept hot until I returned. We sat talking until late into the evening and as I said my goodbyes I was loaded with cigarettes for which they refused any kind of payment and rowed out to Shrimpy with sure knowledge that the fabled hospitality of the desert arabs still exists.

I arrived at El Yadida the next day at about three o'clock. The harbour is tiny and has reefs all round it, but the way in is well marked and, I would say, is a must for all yachts sailing the Moroccan coast. There is a small dinghy club in the harbour that provides showers, water and a bar—and free drinks if you're as lucky as me! One wall of the harbour is also the wall of an old fortified Portugese city, around which the thriving market town of El Yadida has sprung up. The 'old city' is perfectly preserved and is lived in by the poorer people of the town. It is fascinating to walk round the place (free of charge) and actually see the minute shops and houses all occupied—not having to imagine it, as is the case with all the crumbling castles in England. I was enchanted with the place and stayed there for three days, just wandering around.

The next port of call, just a stone's throw down the coast, was the

town of Safi. The town is not exceptional and nor is the port—a large
fishing and commercial concern—but as is so often the case, my visit
was made enjoyable by the hospitality of just one person. Although the
port can provide mooring for any number of yachts there is only one
good berth. This is at the end of the 'club' jetty and it was to here that I
was directed by the Clerk of the club—a young student called
Laghmami Abderrahim who spoke good English.

I invited him aboard and he told me he took an interest in all the
visiting yachts and said I could have free run of the club, which was
mainly patronised by rich Jewish people. There were many small
children in the club and all wanted to come aboard Shrimpy. As I could
not let them all on at once I refused them all until one enterprising lad
offered me a tin of sardines (for which the port is famous) in exchange
for a visit. Well, never let it be said that I won't accept a bribe and, by
the end of the day, Shrimpy was packed with children and sardines!
Before I left I invited Laghmami aboard for a meal and he gave me some
oranges, Moroccan bread (which is delicious), dates, bead necklaces and
leather belts to remember Morocco by. He also told me that I was
moored in the same place as the reed boats *RA I* and *RA II* which
pleased me no end and made little Shrimpy swell with pride.

Now there was just a four-day trip across to my first 'target' port—
Las Palmas, Gran Canaria, from whence I could write 'nose thumbing'
letters to one or two sceptics back in England.

My introduction to the Canaries was very arduous indeed, for soon
after I had left Safi, the wind blew up to gale force from the north-west,
preventing me from steering the course I wanted, and it stayed that way
for four days. I was forced too far south and had to go around the
southern end of the island of Fuerteventura. Here I experienced
tremendous squalls roaring down the mountainside, the like of which I
had never seen before. Then a hard beat across to Gran Canaria still left
me south of Las Palmas, so I ran into the bay (the locals dare to call it a
port) of Arinaga to await calmer weather before attempting to sail the
ten miles or so north to Las Palmas.

Now I had a problem. I had anchored half a mile from shore because
of reefs and the large swell in the bay, and the only food left on board
was a few tins of sardines. I had no dinghy and the fishermen's boats
were all pulled high and dry until the storm ended. There was only one
thing for it, and so, putting my clothes in a plastic bag, I jumped in and
swam ashore checking that my anchors were well dug in on the way.

In all, I spent four days in this very insecure anchorage, swimming
ashore each day to explore and chat to the locals. Out on Shrimpy life
was very uncomfortable, but I found a sheltered nook on the beach, out
of the wind, where I could sit keeping an eye on my boat, and whiling
away the hours until the gale ended. A group of local village girls

became very curious, and each day their pretty, smiling faces would giggle progressively closer to me as they took their regular evening promenade along the beach. By the fourth night three of them, armed with guitars, actually plucked up enough courage to sit beside me, chat to me in sign language and, between giggles, sing many of the romantic Spanish songs to me. By the end of the evening I was half wishing that the gale would go on forever.

By Saturday July 28, the wind had abated to about force six and I decided to try and beat up to Las Palmas. I made it eventually but the ten-mile trip took 14 hours of hard sailing! As I anchored amidst all the other ocean-going yachts, a small dinghy came shooting across to me and I instantly recognised Henri—the man who had asked me to teach him navigation in Falmouth. We had both been worried about each other's ability but we had both made it safe and sound.

I now had to wait in Las Palmas for about three months until the hurricane season ended in the Atlantic and, after all I had heard about the island from travel brochures, I was quite looking forward to my stay. How disappointed I was! Las Palmas harbour is covered with thick oil, the city is very dirty, noisy and smelly, the local people are rude, unhelpful and unfriendly and the Club Nautico—the only place to get ashore—is an absolute disgrace. It was only the fantastic comradeship of all the visiting yachtsmen that made my stay a happy one.

When you first go ashore in Las Palmas you tie your dinghy to the jetty of the Club Nautico and walk through the luxurious premises until you come to the reception desk. Here the secretary gives you a large beautifully bound book and politely asks you to enter into it the particulars of your boat and your voyage. By this time you are thinking what a nice place it is—then comes the shock—you are issued with a pass and are told that you are only allowed to walk through the club to get to and from land. You must show your pass and you cannot take guests out to your boat as they won't be allowed through the club without a pass. You are not allowed to use the bar, the swimming pool, not even the toilets! You cannot slip your boat to clean the bottom no matter what you are prepared to pay. As you explore further ashore, you find that this type of inhospitality is the rule rather than the exception, and you must go right out into the countryside before you meet 'real' people.

Back amongst the yachts, life was much happier and, as I had no money and was looking for work, Henri and Heini invited me to eat with them on *Havglimpt* for a few days, in exchange for the lessons on navigation that I had promised back in England. I now began to meet the people and yachts that were massing to attack 'the crossing'. Amongst them the most memorable were: Stefan—a very large Frenchman, his very small wife, and three small children, on a tiny blue yacht which was covered with chicken wire to stop the children falling overboard. To bath the children, Stefan would pick them up by one arm and wriggle them up and down in the sea! Then there were Sue and Chris on *Easybeat,* now quite happy as I have previously mentioned, but out of funds and, therefore, leaving their boat in Las Palmas while they went back to England to work for a few months. I also met Salvatori—a very gentle soft-spoken American who was working as cook on board a small cargo boat. He had been the owner of the beautiful but ill-fated yacht *Curlew* and after a dreadful experience with a hurricane (see Adlard Coles' *Heavy Weather Sailing*) had not sailed since, until he met Shrimpy. What an honour for my little boat to have such a man at the helm and to help him back to the sea. As I left Las Palmas he had bought a trimaran and was getting it ready for sailing. Finally, there was Camino living on board the yacht *Nina,* who was the only local who took any interest in the visiting yachts and was always ready with kind words and food for any hard-up sailor, although he was not very rich himself.

After a few weeks of lazing around pretending to myself that I was looking for work, a Dane arrived in a dinghy and offered me the job of navigating for him, to Gibraltar, in his beautiful gaff rigged Tahiti ketch, *Dahlia.* I jumped at the chance and we arranged a price for the job that would enable me to store Shrimpy for the 'crossing' when I returned. In all, I worked on *Dahlia* for about a month. It was a very happy ship on the whole and, despite some hard weather sailing and one or two problems, I enjoyed myself immensely but all the time, in the back of my mind, I was anxious about my little boat sitting all alone in the filthy port of Las Palmas and was very pleased when I got back on board her.

By now—November 3—many of the yachts had left and more were arriving from Europe every day. This gave me the chance to meet many more interesting people while I prepared Shrimpy for sea. It was now that I met Cisak Stanislav from Poland on a yacht not much bigger than Shrimpy, called *Narcyz.* We became firm friends and helped each other with food and gear, as we were both quite poor. We had no common language, but with a Polish-English dictionary and much time, we could communicate quite well. Cisak told me how he broke his arm in the middle of the English Channel in mid-winter and how he sailed into Dover in rough weather very literally single-handed!

During this time I was very busy and itching to get underway. I put Shrimpy on the beach and cleaned and painted her between tides. I also decided that I needed a couple of gadgets to make life easier on a long trip. The first thing was to improve the cooking arrangements, for a primus stove wedged between your feet in the cockpit is not the best of ideas in rough seas, especially if you cook chips as often as I do! I buffed up a rusty old biscuit tin found on a rubbish dump, mounted it on a shelf in the cabin and set the primus stove inside it. The whole apparatus I put on gimbals so that the stove would remain upright no matter what the boat did.

I then made a self-steering gear out of old bits of driftwood which I found on the shore, a few nails, some old screws, and a couple of discarded car springs (for the counterbalance). The finished product looked rather crude, but it only took a day to make, cost absolutely nothing, and worked just as well as the professional job which sat on the stern of the nearby yacht, and which I had used as a model. These 'improvements' done, I bought food, water, paraffin, etc, and stowed them all aboard. By Friday November 23 I was ready to go.

I borrowed a dinghy and rowed around the harbour saying goodbye to all my friends who had not yet sailed. Then, with a word of encouragement to Shrimpy I put up the sails and, as we sailed out of the harbour, my mind was already imagining what Barbados would look like, but first there was a bit of water to cross!

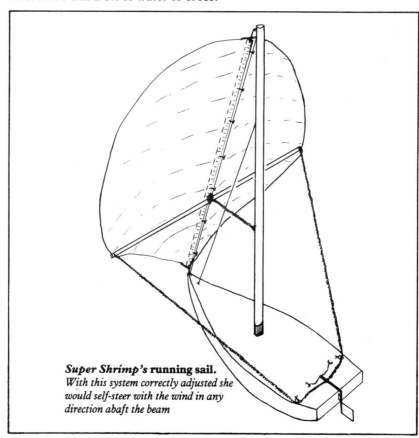

Super Shrimp's **running sail.**
With this system correctly adjusted she would self-steer with the wind in any direction abaft the beam

3

To cross an ocean
November 23 1973–January 3 1974

Day 1

As I sailed out of the harbour, I tried to analyse my feelings but could find no trace of anxiety or fear, no dread of loneliness or distance and no urgency for speed. I think this is because everything becomes so vast that it is impossible to imagine an ocean as a whole and the only way one's mind can come to terms with it is to take each day as a separate voyage. In this way it is easy to see why my feelings were as if I was just out for a day's sail.

About five miles away from the harbour, the wind died completely so I went below and cooked supper. There was still no wind at ten in the evening and so I went to bed disgusted—my log book reads: 'At this rate it will take years'.

Day 3

It was not until noon on the third day that I eventually got some wind and managed to lose sight of the Canaries. The wind was from the south at about force four, which meant my first chance to fiddle with the self-steering gear which I had made, in order to try and get it to work. This gear was a really rough job knocked together in an afternoon with galvanised nails and a few bits of driftwood, and weighted with a couple of old springs, but the principle was good and after a few extra bits of string had been added, I got it going perfectly! This was a great relief for it meant that the boat would now give maximum performance automatically no matter which direction the wind.

Day 4

By this time, I was beginning to settle down to life at sea and so, thank heavens, was my stomach. Shrimpy was sailing herself all the time and I was reading or writing, listening to the radio or just watching the sea. The meals I cooked were becoming more elaborate as I returned myself to the motion of the sea and, from my meagre stores, 'beautiful' dishes were conjured up, tasting all the better for the surroundings of clear sky and sea. Suddenly, straight out of the blue, came my first problem—the radio stopped. This was serious, for without regular time checks from the BBC world service, I would not be able to find my longitude because my watch—a very cheap one—was extremely erratic,

31

gaining or losing as much as five seconds an hour! The radio had to be fixed, but I am no electrician and had no spares or tools. I reasoned that, being a solid-state transistor, the radio (a cheap Japanese one) could not have much wrong with it as there are very few moving parts. So, after much technical thought, I got out my toothbrush and gave it a good scrub. This, believe it or not, had the desired effect and the radio sprang to life again. I concluded that it was the salty atmosphere which was the culprit.

Day 6

I had been making fairly slow progress as the wind was all very light and mainly from the south. So I got out my sextant, for the first time, to find exactly how far I had gone. My estimated distance was 380 miles and I found my true distance was 420 miles. This was an unexpectedly pleasant surprise as I always tend to over-estimate and my log reads: 'celebrated with souffle omelettes for supper'.

Day 8

Shrimpy was still sailing quite happily, if slowly, when suddenly at 11 at night—*bang*! She went right over on her side, chucking me out of my bunk. A large squall had hit us from the south-west. I scrambled on deck and crawled to the bow to get the sails down. It was quite a struggle even with the small size sails Shrimpy carries. Once or twice I lost my footing and had reason to bless my safety harness and the fact that I wear it constantly. Once the sails were off her, Shrimpy was much happier, although far from comfortable, laying sideways on to the swell and being covered with water every five minutes or so. There was only one thing I could do—tie myself to the bunk, shut all the hatches and go to sleep. These violent squalls lasted all night and all through the next day. I just had to let Shrimpy drift at the mercy of the sea as it would be too dangerous to put up any sail.

Day 10

I woke to find the sea quite smooth with a gentle wind from the south—still no sign of the famous north-east trade winds—so I got the sails up and off we went again. I discovered that I was now a quarter of the way across, so I checked all stores and water to find that I had used about a fifth; I celebrated with an extra large lunch.

Day 12

The wind, at last, went round to east and I was able to set my running sail for the first time! The radio had become more and more troublesome and I was having to nurse it very carefully— putting in a new battery each time I used it and only having it turned on long enough to get a time check.

I was beginning to see more and more flying fish but found, to my dismay, that very few landed on my boat at night and mainly only the ones which were too small to eat. This was disappointing as I had had

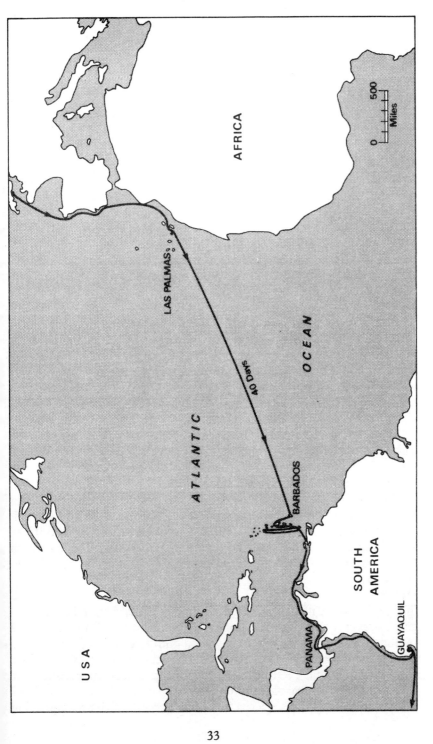

visions of big plump fish jumping straight into the frying pan. I also had a lure towing along, but caught nothing all the way across.

Day 15

The wind went back to south and began to blow quite hard, about force six, which meant only a small jib sail and very slow progress. Then, as I was looking around at about ten in the morning, I saw a massive thundercloud creeping up on me and, to my horror, at the centre of this cloud was a massive column of water which extended right down to the surface of the sea. A waterspout! And à giant one at that. Now, I have read that these things are not dangerous and can be collapsed merely by sticking a boathook into them. But after one look at this awesome monster, I wasn't going to hang around to find out. All day I hightailed it away from the spout, not caring about my course as long as it was away from this phenomenon. Eventually, it passed me about half a mile astern and I was very surprised that I experienced no exceptional winds or seas as it did so. After watching it depart and thanking it for missing me, I turned back on to the right course and set Shrimpy on 'automatic' once again.

Day 19

The wind up to this time was still all wrong and mainly from the south, about force three. The radio was still hanging on by the skin of its teeth, but little Shrimpy was gamely ploughing on and my daily crosses on the chart by now extended almost halfway across the ocean. I went to bed quite content. At about midnight, however, I heard a horrible grinding noise coming from outside the hull. My first reaction (idiotic as it seems now) was to jump to the chart table and look at the depths given— thinking I had grounded in mid-ocean! This, of course, was not the case, so I picked up the torch and went on deck to have a look. What I saw really scared me. A great shark—easily as long as Shrimpy—scratching itself against her hull.

After thinking for a while, I decided it was best to keep quite still and quiet instead of trying to scare him away, because if he got angry it could easily be the end of me. After what seemed like an eternity of silent waiting, with my heart pounding, he went away, leaving me to have a rather disturbed sleep, dreaming of horrible Shrimpy-eating creatures.

Day 20

The radio had by now become the focal point of my day, so I decided to stop nursing it and give it 'kill or cure' treatment which meant a good toothbrushing, some vicious shaking and bumping, a bit of screwdriver poking and a lot of swearing. After all this, amazingly, I had no further trouble with it and even managed to pick up Radio Australia's short wave broadcast for two days on the run.

Later in the day, I discovered that I had two pilot fish accompanying me and spent all afternoon amusing myself by throwing little titbits out to them. They seemed to get so full that it was a struggle for them to keep up with Shrimpy who was blistering along at about two miles per hour.

Day 25

Half-way across the Atlantic and the trade winds had arrived! I was quite elated and, of course, celebrated with an outsize lunch. Then checked the quantity and quality of the stores and water; everything was in good condition and only about a third gone.

After 25 days at sea I was still feeling as fit and healthy as when I left Las Palmas. There were no pangs of loneliness or fear, I knew my little boat was sound and happy; I felt at one with my environment and was beginning to see why Bernard Moitessier—my hero—had said to hell with the money I'm continuing in order to 'save my soul', when he pulled out of his leading position in the Round the World race and sailed on.

Time was beginning to lose importance; my food and water were lasting better than I expected and the only reason I bothered to keep track of the date was for my navigation. Life was beautiful as Shrimpy and I slowly sailed on light trade winds towards the sunset in the daytime and towards Venus at night.

Day 32

Christmas Day and presents for everyone! Who? Well, *Super Shrimp* was given some varnish, my pilot fish got extra rations, the sea and the sky were wished a Happy Christmas. And for me? Well, a big meal of course (the number of times I find reason to eat well is amazing) and two aural treats from Auntie Beeb in the form of the unique Tony Hancock and the Goon Show. On the more philosophical side of Christmas, it was this day in the middle of the Atlantic that I was finally able to put my thoughts on religion into words and my thinking is as follows: I am sure there are greater, more intelligent powers in this universe than man—you can label these powers God if you like—but I am equally sure that these powers are totally unconcerned, more probably totally unaware of the insignificant creatures called homosapiens on the insignificant planet called Earth revolving around the totally insignificant star called the Sun in this tiny galaxy of ours. Therefore, to my mind, it is ridiculous to pray to these powers or God in the hope of an afterlife. All we can do is enjoy our short span of awareness to the full before we return to the nothingness from whence we came. If you disagree then go sail an ocean and may be you will see what I mean.

Day 33

Boorrrrh! Boorrrrh! Boorrrrh! That was the noise that woke me early in the morning. Bloody motorists I thought and turned over to go back to sleep. Boorrrrh! Boorrrrh! Boorrrrh! This time I was fully awake. I jumped up and opened the hatch. *Rust!* No sky, no sea, just *rust!* I slammed the hatch shut again and shivered with fright. I must still be dreaming. I inched the hatch open again and looked up and up and up—to the bridge of a large cargo ship! This was *Ciudad Menzales* of Cartagena and the Captain had skillfully manoeuvred his ship alongside to make sure I was OK. I told him everything was fine and that I was in need of nothing. So, with a wave from the rather astonished crew lining the rails, they sailed out of sight. Although it was very considerate of the Captain to stop his ship to check on me, I'm afraid my initial reaction was, 'What's this thing doing in my bit of sea, spoiling the scenery', and I may have appeared a bit churlish to them.

Day 38
This was 'navigation day'—the daily position of crosses on the chart had now stretched right across the ocean with only a small gap between the last one and the island of Barbados. I found that I could transfer the last cross on to the larger scale chart of the West Indies. I was, however, quite anxious as there is no way of checking your navigation at sea, and the more I thought about it the surer I became that it is impossible to find out where you are with nothing more than a couple of mirrors (sextant) and a book of tables. So I took about ten sights at different times throughout the day. They all agreed within a few miles and I worked out that by 4.30 pm the next evening I should see land.

Day 39
All that day I was tense with excitement, always peering ahead although pretending to myself that I was looking for nothing in particular. Finally, the magic time of 4.30 arrived and I stared and stared—*nothing*. Looking back it is, of course, ridiculous to hope for that kind of accuracy but, at the time, I was really disappointed as I had been so keyed up. My immediate reaction (typically English) was to go below and make a cup of tea. When I emerged ten minutes later—cup in hand—I glanced forward and saw land—*land—Barbados*!! We had made it and emotions of all kinds pulsed through me: I was jumping up and down screaming and shouting, then keeping ice cool with a slight, confident smile, weeping, laughing, patting my boat and whispering endearments, sitting quietly and calmly knowing it had been inevitable all along, high, low, happy, sad, feeling nothing, feeling everything. It was very strange, for never before have I felt emotions as powerful as this—not even in my 'first love' type romances. I now put the sextant and compass away, unhooked the self-steering and sat at the tiller throughout the night beneath the warm tropical skies full of bright stars, trailing one hand in the sea watching the phosphorescence sparkling as Shrimpy skipped along with a bone in her teeth, southwards around the Island and into the harbour of Bridgetown.

4

In steel band lands
January 3–July 1 1974

The harbour at Bridgetown Barbados is called the Careenage and although very well protected from the sea it is very small and full of local fishing boats and trading ships, so as soon as I had cleared customs, I sailed back out into the bay to moor amidst the other yachts off the local yacht club.

As usual, I had arrived broke and was on my last packet of cigarettes. I thought that this would be no problem, however, as I could make a bit of money by selling my story to the paper and the local radio—I hadn't reckoned on Jeff! He was an Australian who had arrived in a small boat a few days before me and his boat, although a couple of feet longer than mine, had one small difference—no cabin! It was a 'Drascombe Longboat' and he had had quite a crossing, taking over 50 days, running into bad weather and out of food and water. Compared to this craft, Shrimpy was a palace.

There was also another boat a bit longer than Shrimpy but with much less living space—a Scottish fishing boat of about 21 foot and believe it or not, flush decked! On top of this, there was not one but two people on board. The boat was *The Aegre,* owned by Nick and Julie. They had gone up to Scotland especially to build the boat, so it was not until after three or four days of chatting to each other that I discovered that we (or our parents) live only about two miles from each other back in Cambridge.

With no money and the possibility of getting a job on the island seeming pretty remote, I was beginning to feel down and was sitting on the boat wondering what to do when two guys swam out to chat. They were Italians who were roaming around hitch-hiking on various yachts and whom I had already met in Las Palmas. Although not very rich, they had some money and asked if they could charter Shrimpy to go sailing around the Grenadine Islands. There she was again—Lady Luck—dead on cue. The terms of the charter were simplicity themselves—as long as they fed me and kept me in cigarettes we would sail whenever, wherever and for as long as they liked. This suited them down to the ground so Francesco and Pino joined Shrimpy and we sailed that evening. We were bound first for the port of Fort de France on the southern end of Martinique but, because of the extra weight on board, my calculations on leeway, etc, were so much adrift that before we knew it we were much too far north and had to sail right around the island to get there. This made Francesco and Pino certain I had reached Barbados from Las Palmas more by luck than judgement. From Fort de France (more of that later) we sailed southwards exploring the bays and coves of Martinique—the most beautiful of all the Windward Islands—and eventually found ourselves in the town of St Anne. Here we were offered $100 US to sail to the island of St Lucia and return with a cargo of 100 shirts (made from flour sacks and sold to tourists at ridiculous prices). Needless to say, we sailed instantly!

On arrival at Port Castries, I ran into trouble, for St Lucia* is an island of red tape and petty, pompous officials and, if you are travelling by boat, should definitely be avoided. The trouble is that they charge you, not for mooring, not for use of facilities, not for harbour dues, but merely for clearing customs. They also charge overtime, not for the time you actually clear but for the time you enter the harbour and the charge is £3. They also charge you for leaving the port! I was astonished for two reasons. Firstly, every other port in the Windward Isles charges nothing and welcomes any small-boat adventurer, as indeed do most other countries in the world (outside Europe). Secondly, I couldn't afford it. So I said to the official:

'I'm sorry, I didn't realise there was a charge so we'll leave straight away and not go ashore'.

'Oh no', he said, 'You can't leave until you've paid and you can't stay until you've paid either.'

What beautiful bureaucracy!

I got mad—I walked straight to the Governor's house and demanded justice. From there I was passed from official to official, creating havoc as I went until eventually it was agreed that, if we left the island *toute suite* they would forget they had seen us. By this time, however, in between 'official' interviews, I had sold an article to the local newspaper and also been given some money by some very generous tourists who had heard of our plight. So with a nice innocent smile on my face I walked back to the office and said, 'I have money now; I would like to pay and stay, please'. This caused even more trouble and ill-feeling as these officials now had to find all the forms they had carefully cancelled or hidden. It is easy to beat them at their own game because you can make your rules up as you go along but they have to keep to a narrow (red taped) line.

While Francesco and Pino were rounding-up the flour sack shirts, I

---

* Author's note: St Lucia had not yet gained independence when I visited it, perhaps things are different now.

was meeting locals round the docks—notably Brownie who could talk the hind legs off a donkey, in the nicest possible way, and also the English crews from the Cunard and Geest boats who were very generous with food and gear for my little boat.

It was a happy coincidence that the *QE II* arrived on the same day that my article and photograph appeared in the local paper. Tying my boat at a strategic point, I bought a great wad of newspapers and sold them at a large profit—with my signature across the photograph—to all those generous American tourists.

Back in the Island of Martinique, we collected our $100 for the shirts—$33 each—and moved a mile down the coast to pull Shrimpy high and dry on to the golden sandy beach of the Club Méditerranée—a back-to-nature-with-trimmings type hotel. We did this in the depth of night so if told to move we would have at least six hours' grace (until the tide came in) to nose around. As it happened, we had picked the centre of the nudist section of the beach, which gave me quite a shock when in the early hours of the morning (about ten o'clock) I crawled out of the cabin and, instead of seeing blue sea as was my wont, could see nothing but frying flesh!

The sailing instructors and others at the Club proved very friendly; no one tried to move us and someone managed to sneak us a bucket full of fantastic fruits, cheeses, meats, etc, every day. Also, there were many available girls—sadly very few were attractive. We were very loth to leave this temporary paradise but the call of the Grenadine Islands was strong and for the next two weeks we sailed around this 'yachting playground' visiting islands large and small, inhabited and virgin, attractive and ugly. We got on very well together—you have to, three in an 18-foot boat—swimming, spear fishing and barbecuing the catch on a deserted beach. Eating local foods that we had never seen before, chatting to the natives and amongst ourselves, visiting other yachts from all over the globe were our main activities. The only bad time was when Pino innocently ate half a dozen machinele fruits which are very poisonous, but after two or three days on a diet of milk and sugar (the local remedy) he recovered quickly.

We sailed to Kingstown, St Vincent, in time for 'carnival' and I saw, for the first time, the fabled steel bands and calypso singers. Even on a comparatively small island such as St Vincent the spectacle was unbelievable; the combination of solid simple unpretentious music and cheap potent rum, makes you feel very good, to put it mildly. On February 25, Francesco and Pino left for Italy, after a memorable, if somewhat unusual, charter. Although I now had sufficient money for my immediate needs, I would need a bit more before I could sail on and decided that Martinique would be the best place to earn it, so without further ado, I sailed back to Fort de France.

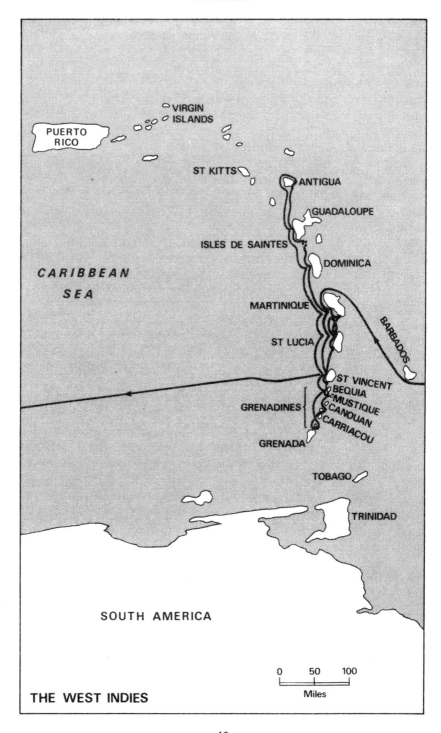

THE WEST INDIES

This island is the main port in the Windward Islands for tourist boats, bringing in many thousands of American tourists each week. Also, the natives of Fort de France are very affluent so, while looking for work, I moored alongside the main jetty and put a large sign on my boat saying (in English), 'Sailed single-handed from England'. On the shore, I placed a board to which I pinned a newspaper article of my adventures and a sign saying, 'Please help me sail around the world'. Beneath this, I placed a small collection box. To my amazement, I no longer had to look for a job. I could work on my boat all the time, pausing every few minutes to smile at a camera, or answer a few questions and earn about £5 a day. I thank you all a thousand times for your undoubted generosity, interest and wishes of luck—but please please don't ask me any more if I anchor each night at sea, or have a radio-telephone on board. (For landlubbers, the answer to both is *no*.)

Whilst anchored here I met hundreds of interested and interesting people and became somewhat of a celebrity. Most visiting yachts had heard of me before they met me; wherever I went in town people knew of me. I was quite overcome by it all. Quite apart from my overflowing collecting box, generosity poured in. Felix Ramion, the local 'flying dutchman' king mended all my sails. Chantal, one of the prettiest girls I have ever seen, brought me food and drinks and friendship. There were also unforgettable weekends spend with Mr and Mrs Paul Radiguet and their seven children, in the town of Vauchin where Paul, a Frenchman, was working. I could continue in this vein for hours. Thank you Martinique.

My feet were getting itchy again and so on April 8 I began sailing up and down the islands seeing the sights and meeting old and new friends. Notably Chris and Sue of *Easybeat* who had made a very fast crossing and both had got jobs in St Lucia. Sailing up and down the Windward Isles is not the 'yachting paradise' it is cracked up to be. Between the islands you usually have to beat into a sloppy sea no matter whether you are heading north or south and in the lee of the islands the wind blows from all directions or none, with squalls belting down from the mountains. In the rain showers it gets very cold and visibility is nil. All the beautiful charter boats very rarely move under sails alone—which is very sad. By Sunday May 12, I found myself in St Vincent once more and was now ready to sail across to the Venezuelan coast and the Dutch Island of Curacao. Of all the Caribbean islands I had visited, I found that the French ones are by far the best by any standards—it is sad for me, as an Englishman, to have to say this but it is undoubtedly true.

I left St Vincent feeling rather low as I had just been talking to some 'Sunday sailors' who had been telling me of the perils of the Caribbean Sea—although I knew full well that these self-styled 'experts' had never been out of sight of land. It was depressing. The weather wasn't helping much either, a drizzly, gusty day with a high, confused swell. As soon as I cleared the lee of the island, however, things improved immediately and with strong wind and current behind me Shrimpy was racing along at top speed—it was good to be alone with the sea and the sky once more.

Throughout the next four days the sailing was fast and exhilarating and I reached the Dutch island of Bonaire in very high spirits. Bonaire is rather a dull place but the town is very pretty and very Dutch. The island is famous for its flamingoes and infamous for the ridiculous outpourings of a large, evangelistic radio station.

Almost as soon as I tied up, I was invited to a shower by a Dutch yachtsman and his wife, who, on this their third Atlantic crossing, were settling down for a few years on the island. Later in the evening, I was invited to a party by the same couple, which lasted well into the next morning—so I was quite amazed to find myself sailing for Curacao by eight o'clock. The wind was very strong and the sea very high, but still all dead astern, and it only took about eight hours to reach the yacht harbour of 'Spanish Water', Curacao. Having no chart of the harbour, I immediately ran aground on a reef (the water not being very clear), but I was towed off at once by a local yacht owner, who lent me his secure berth at the local yacht club. Spanish Water is a beautiful lagoon with a narrow entrance, but there is usually too much wind for comfort. It is also a long way from town, so after a few days I sailed down the coast to Willemstad harbour and moored right in the centre of the town.

Curacao struck me as very European, very affluent and very uninteresting, with the exception of an old pontoon bridge at the entrance to the harbour. This bridge is constantly rolling and pitching in the heavy swell but in spite of this it has a tarmac surface which seems to stay in reasonable condition! I stayed in Curacao for about a week waiting for my mail to catch up with me—there was nothing else of interest to keep me there although the locals were friendly and helpful.

My next port was to be Santa Marta in Columbia. As I neared the mainland the wind and sea gradually moderated, making for really pleasant sailing. Late at night, I was resting inside the cabin when Shrimpy hit something pretty hard and gave me quite a start. I leaped out of the cabin to find myself alongside a Venezuelan fishing boat with one of its crew members hanging on to Shrimpy's rigging and smiling. As soon as he saw me emerge, he quickly let go and fishing boat sped off into the night. I can only assume that they thought Shrimpy was adrift and they had got themselves a salvage prize and were quite startled when I popped out. Luckily Shrimpy suffered only superficial damage and it was safe to carry on sailing. The following afternoon the elements put on a glorious display—the sea turned the colour of pea soup (the effect of a large river, although I was well out of sight of land) and went quite flat and calm. At the same time, the sky went pure pink, a very dense, even colour all over the sky. This combination of really intense colouring made for a completely alien environment and it was easy to imagine that I was on another planet altogether.

The next four days were spent in calm and frustration as I ran out of cigarettes, food and matches. So miserable I became that I found myself rolling cigarettes made from the contents of teabags, wrapped in toilet paper and lighting these with one of my emergency flares!

Eventually wind returned and I sailed into Santa Marta, Columbia. I had planned to stay there for two or three days but, during the first day the famous Columbian thieves struck three times and I sailed out the same day—minus radio, watch and binoculars—in a very bad mood. I decided to head straight for Panama, but King Neptune had different ideas and chucked some really fierce weather at me, ripping a couple of sails and forcing me into the port of Cartagena for a day of sewing. I sailed the next day in ideal conditions and, after four days good sailing, I sighted the coast of Panama and immediately the wind died completely. I was left to drift aimlessly up and down the coast at the whim of the currents for three days, all the time slowly edging nearer to the dangerous Archipelago de las Mulatas! My line of drift was straight towards a very small island of about two acres and about three feet above sea level. It looked beautiful but the reefs prevented me from entering the lagoon, so I anchored outside in the rough swell to wait for some wind. Help was at hand, however, for out over the reef came a dugout canoe full of Cuna Indians, one of whom actually spoke reasonable English! They took my little boat in tow through a narrow gap in the reefs and I anchored just off their homestead. They took me ashore and showed me their island. Just two families live on it and earn a reasonable income selling lobsters to the mainland. Their houses and all their everyday utensils were made from palm trees and the only things they required that had to be bought were outboard motors, clothes, cigarettes and radios, despite easy access to the mainland.

As my food supply was getting low, I asked to buy some bananas and coconuts and offered them an American dollar—this bought as much food as I could carry (and more, if I had had the space). It also bought all the cooked meals I wanted during my three days' stay on this glorious little islet. With the return of favourable wind I said goodbye to my small Red Indian friends—all under five feet tall—and continued along the Panama coastline, stopping overnight in the pretty little port of Miramar, and the next morning I sailed into the port of Cristobal, entrance to the Panama Canal and the Pacific Ocean! I could see only one yacht there, but one was enough, for it was none other than *Havglimpt* with Henri and Heini still aboard!

5

An Iris blooms in Panama
July 1–August 15 1974

The yacht anchorage in Cristobal harbour is appalling, filthy dirty water, very rough and exposed and a good mile away from the only permitted landing spot. Furthermore, because of some ridiculous law, you are not allowed to use a motor on your dinghy, but must row ashore, all the time dodging in and out of the continually moving tugs and ships. I would guess that a trip across Cristobal harbour in a dinghy is ten times as dangerous as a trip across an ocean in a yacht! Admittedly there is better anchorage at the yacht club but this is very expensive and often unavailable. The yacht club is, however, as helpful as possible, working within the stupid amount of red tape in the port. It also has a 24-hour bar!

It was in this bar that Henri, Heini and myself celebrated our reunion and toasted our two brave little craft which had crossed the Atlantic and safely met on its western shore. Our conversation then turned to the future. Heini had decided to go off to South America to explore the Amazon. Henri and I had many plans but little money, and Henri also had two friends who wanted to sail, so we decided to go back to visit my Red Indian friends once more, after, of course, seeing Heini off on his adventure.

A couple of days later, I set sail back to the St Blas islands after having given Henri very complicated instructions on how to find the islet of 'my' Red Indians amongst the 150 or so other similar islets of the Mulatas Archipelago. I had not even got out of the harbour, however, before I was waylaid by a shout of, 'We've got cold beer!' from an English freighter. Handing my bow line to a willing crew member, I scrambled up the side and dived straight into the crew's mess room. About an hour later one of the watchmen came down and calmly said, 'Is that your yacht on the other side of the harbour?' I rushed on deck and sure enough Shrimpy had gone adrift and was almost ready to smash into the harbour wall. I was furious at the crew for not having tied a decent knot and furious at myself for not having checked it and thought, 'Well, here it all ends', but the crew of the ship, anxious to prove their seamanship, launched their lifeboat in record time and saved Shrimpy from an ignoble death.

Without further mishap, I rejoined *Havglimpt* in the lagoon of 'my' islet and renewed the friendship of the two families there. After a few idle days together, Henri decided to sail off to Costa Rica; I would visit some more of these islands, taking with me his two friends. So, once again, Shrimpy was full. Of my new 'crew' one was Chris, a wandering Frenchman who took to paying his way by getting up early, donning mask, flippers and spear gun and not returning until he had caught enough lobster for us all. The other was Iris Derungs, a beautiful blonde-haired, blue-eyed, Swiss girl who had rarely even seen the sea let alone sailed on it, but who was quite an adventurous person in her own right, having amongst other things, walked across the Sudan by herself living with any of the wandering tribes of Massai who she met on the way, discretely purifying the water they drank (which is poisonous for Europeans in its natural form) and somehow managing to eat the food they offered which, to them, was presumably delicious.

Iris writes: 'The first time I set eyes on Shrimpy, I saw her surrounded by a glorious sheen of adventure. Painted a sun yellow, the colour of a wanderer, the inside was fitted out with no more than the basic necessities of life. Blankets stiff with salt told the story of rough seas, unimaginable on this beautiful sunny day, and anyway my ideas of gales stemmed solely from books and films. Now, after long wanderings through bush, steppes, and desert, it was the water which called to me.

'Perhaps Panama seems a long way to come from my Swiss mountains to seek adventure at sea, but it so happened that I wanted to meet some of my friends there whom I had not seen for many years. However, I am not chained to any set plan or pattern and whenever something attractive crosses my path I can say yes. Now it was yes to Shrimpy.

'Shane, the Captain, was already known to me as a mysterious and heroic figure through the gossip of other 'yachties' in the port who, like fishermen, tended to tell stories which would turn minnows into whales. Curious by nature, I wanted to meet this person. Today I know why the stories took on such a shape; Shane is a quiet man, he is more of an introvert than an extrovert, he doesn't need to conjure small gales into hurricanes, he doesn't need any certain type of clothing to express his image; when I met him all he owned was a pair of oilskin trousers, many sizes too big, a problem he had overcome with a few old bits of rope! That he was very contented with the type of life he was living was obvious because his whole being exuded peace, so as well as 'yes' to Shrimpy it was also 'yes' to Shane!'

As we sailed through these beautiful St Blas islets, the need for a dinghy became great, so we bought one—an old dugout canoe about as long and as heavy as Shrimpy herself, very leaky and with only an inch of freeboard. Towing this behind us cut our speed by half, but we had nowhere we needed to go in a hurry anyway. Eventually we arrived at a group of three islets close together which made up the main village of the Indians, and what a strange sight it was! Originally, for protection from Columbian pirates the Indians had grouped themselves close together and remained on these three islets as the population grew. So, today, there is not even room for one tree or even a blade of grass. There are no roads, of course, and even the footpaths are 'one-way'! Surprisingly enough, in spite of all this overcrowding, the people are peaceful, happy and scrupulously clean. Each day fleets of canoes leave the village in search of food and water and it is a wonderful sight to watch them flat out under sail, fanning out over the horizon.

Iris writes: 'How incredibly different life is when spent on an island which you can circumnavigate in five minutes. Standing on its edge you find your eyes taking in the whole island without moving your head. Very soon you know every single tree, the direction of the prevailing winds, the shadiest spots, which coconut is at just the right stage of ripeness to provide the most refreshing drink, all the little paths made by the ants, a new spider's web is a surprise, visits from seabirds make you aware of the sky. On these tiny, sandy, corally islands there are not many flowers, so every shade of green through to brown, backlit by the shimmering, blinding white of the sand, are the main colours to be found, but from dawn to dusk as the sun rolls round the sky, you can paint a different picture every few minutes of the endlessly changing hues and shades. Frequently the sunset at close of day will tint the sky with rainbow colours and then the coconuts take on such an unimaginable garb of vibrating pigments that all the fashions made by man can never hope to match.

'It looked as if these tiny islands had also shaped their peoples, even the size of their bodies was in proportion; a mere four feet tall. What nature had omitted in the way of colours was provided by the women, who made beautifully decorated clothing, this being one of the many handicrafts which they were able to do while lazing in their hammocks underneath a cool coconut-leaf roof inside their huts. The days' movements were slow and peaceful, punctuated by chatter and laughter. I was shocked to discover that this happy rhythm of life could be completely disrupted by the cries of a child, the whole community would be concerned about his sorrow, taking time to soothe him and cheer him up, not by promises of 'goodies' but just by the simple, genuine smiles which are always so close at hand. How easy it was to smile with them once away from the pace of European life.'

One evening we were invited to a dance in their main village hall and watched enthralled for, as the band (two flutes) wailed a mournful chant, the dancers set a contrastingly lively rhythm with much stamping of feet and jingling of hundreds of paper-thin pure gold necklaces. When it came to our turn to join in the dancing, we had to do so bent double—so small are these people and so low are the ceilings of their houses.

A while later we headed back along the mainland coast towards Cristobal. Our poor canoe—which we were still towing, for we would need it to get ashore when we arrived—developed more and more leaks, so I decided to stop at Portobello to fix it. Anchoring in nice calm water, we left Chris to his fishing and paddled ashore. The idea was to tar the canoe's bottom, so Iris and I spent a few hours wandering along the road picking up every bit of loose tar we came across. When we had a nice big sack full, we returned to the canoe to find that the sea had got quite choppy. Iris was sure that the canoe would never get me, her and the tar back to Shrimpy, but bowed to my greater knowledge of the sea. Halfway out we sank! This earned one the honoured title of Dinghy Captain which, to this day, still hurts. When we eventually reached Shrimpy Iris, still in her mood of humorous vengeance, told Chris that our cargo was not tar but steak cutlets (the one thing he drooled about). So well did she play her part that, until he reads these words, he will call me in all sincerity Dinghy Captain!

A few days later, Chris decided to leave us (maybe to go and eat some cutlets) and Iris and I continued coast-hopping towards Cristobal. We were about ten miles away from the harbour when the wind died away and we began to drift dangerously near to the coral reef which fringes this part of the coast. Wondering what to do, I suddenly spied a tiny passage wandering in through the reef and decided to give it a try. We made it, but only just, and ended up in a little sandy lagoon of about 20 yards in diameter. In front of us, carved out of the dense jungle, was an acre of mown grass good enough for a cricket field. In the middle of the field was a square brick house and surrounding it was a circular structure of metal and wire resembling a radio aerial or telescope around which were signs saying 'Keep Out'. We kept out and were quite content to stay on the boat or the sand or in the water and wait for the wind to return. Suddenly we found ourselves surrounded by US Marines pointing loaded rifles at us! It turned out that this was a Top Secret something or other (they didn't even know what). There was no pass through the reef (officially surveyed), so what were we doing there? Were we Russian? Would we leave immediately? I courteously explained how we came to be there and that, to the best of my knowledge, the Russians don't make 18-foot, ocean-going spy ships!

After a while we all calmed down and became quite friendly and the Marines even shared their meals with us as our supplies were getting low. A few days later, while we were still waiting for enough wind to sail, a very agitated officer arrived and told us that the next day some of the Top Brass would be arriving to inspect the place and would start laying eggs if they saw Shrimpy happily anchored there. A solution was found. The customs officers were called and drove us into Cristobal where, with a bit of slight official pressure, someone was found willing to lend us an outboard motor. We were then driven back to Shrimpy and the motor was fixed to her stern. 'Now off you go', they said. By this time, we discovered that a beautiful breeze had sprung up so, with a wave of farewell, we put the cover on the engine and sailed calmly out through the pass. I have a feeling that if you sailed there today you would find a concrete wall, mines, submarines and God knows what barring your access to this beautiful anchorage.

Returning to Cristobal harbour we had an easy sail. It was a beautiful day. As I looked around me I knew I had everything I wanted—the warm sun, blue sky, calm clear sea, a brave little boat and a beautiful, lovable girl. Yes, Iris had become part of my dream, my adventure, my paradise. With high hopes, I asked her to sail with me across the Pacific and to my delight and amazement she said 'Yes'.

We had to spend about a month in Cristobal's horrible anchorage getting Shrimpy ready and waiting for mail and money to catch us up. During all this time, the only way to get ashore was by using our canoe (still unrepaired and leaking even more). We discovered that we could only get ashore when the harbour was flat calm and if, while ashore, the wind got up we had no idea if we could return the same day or even the same week! This put severe restraint on our social activities.

During this time of waiting I was once again surprised by generosity. This time, not by individual people, but by the International Yacht Paints Company who, having heard about Shrimpy, had agreed to supply all her paint free of charge—not only here in Panama but anywhere throughout the world whenever she needed it. This eventually involved telegrams, air freight and many many problems, but they never gave up and never forgot. For me this was perfect for I had always used this paint in the past and found it amazingly good. Needless to say, I will continue to use it in the future.

Eventually Iris, Shrimpy and I were ready to attempt the Canal. We arranged everything from finding a towing boat—for we had no engine—to signing a paper promising that little Shrimpy would not damage the locks! The day before we started, a small tug-boat pulling a massive oil derrick, anchored nearby and invited us aboard for a drink. This turned into several and, by that evening, we had rope, fish hooks, almanacs, etc, etc, and they had a real, genuine, leaky dugout canoe!

Our tow through the Canal was to be by a beautiful old black schooner called *Bagheera* with a happy young crew aboard. The Canal is about 50 miles long with three locks at each end. It may not look much from the decks of a large ship but from Shrimpy it was awe-inspiring, especially at night when the whole length of the Canal is lit

Above Super Shrimp. **Below left** *Shane Acton*. **Below right** *Iris Derungs*.

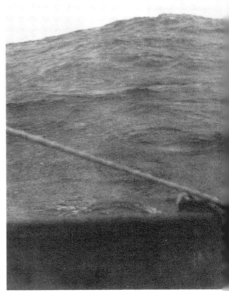

SHRIMPY

Far left *Shrimpy sets out across the Atlantic, the first long leg of the voyage.*

Left *The self-steering gear hard at work.*

Below far left *Mid-Atlantic, Shrimpy's running sail is pulling her happily along.*

Below left *Large ocean swells constantly obscure the horizon.*

Right *Beached in the Caribbean— time for a repaint.*

Below *Unfortunately I don't have a radio room. I don't even have a radio!*

THE PANAMA CANAL

SHIP IDENTIFICATION NUMBER

172154

KEEP THIS CARD IN THE RADIO ROOM.
YOU MUST REPORT THIS NUMBER ON ALL ARRIVAL
MESSAGES FOR TRANSITS OR PORT CALLS.

PRESIDENT, PANAMA CANAL COMPANY

Above *In Panama Iris tentatively takes the tiller for the first time.* **Below left** *The storm clouds begin to build, always an eerie time at sea and even more so here in mid-Pacific.* **Below right** *Shrimpy sits in Papeete harbour, Tahiti, looking very scruffy after her long voyage across the Pacific.*

with lights pointing outwards on to the banks (so as not to dazzle the navigator). Additional red and green flashing navigational lights turn the whole place into a fairyland—a tropical fairyland—for above all is the overwhelming noise of the jungle, the smell of intense dampness and the water rushing past the boat. Quite an experience. The only dangerous parts of the Canal, for a yacht, are its locks. Here, the speed at which the water is raised or lowered, plus the churning screws of the large ships in the lock with you, sets up an enormous amount of turbulence and the mooring lines require constant attention. Thanks mainly to the expert seamanship of the crew of our towing yacht both Shrimpy and *Bagheera* made it safely through without a scratch.

Iris couldn't see what all the fuss was about, but you can imagine my excitement when the last great door of the last great lock was opened and Shrimpy sailed out into the waters of a completely new ocean, so far from England. It was hard for me to believe that here I was afloat in the Pacific. We anchored for the night next to a French tuna fishing boat and were invited aboard for a meal which included delicious French bread and wine. Soon after we were back on board Shrimpy, one of our host ship's powerboats accidentally ploughed into our stern, snapping the mast backstay and splintering a bit of plywood. The crew were so upset that they showered us with gifts, repaired Shrimpy and also sent over their top net maker who made us pre-shaped nylon nets for various nooks and crannies in the boat to assist our storage space. So well were they made that they are still in position today.

The next morning it was time for us to say goodbye to everyone and set out to see what the Pacific had in store for us. I decided that to try and do one long leg through the doldrums to the Galapogos Islands would probably take too long for comfort, so we would sail down the coast of South America to Ecuador against the currents, but near to land so we could anchor whenever we got fed up and needed a bit of a rest. This would also give Iris a chance to get used to sailing before we attempted the longish Ecuador-Galapogos passage. Another reason was that we didn't really have enough money or stores to get us all the way to Tahiti (the next major port) and hoped to find some work in Ecuador. With all this in mind we took our first tentative steps out into the Pacific.

6

The South American way
August 15–December 24 1974

Guayaquil, the main port of Ecuador is only about 700 miles away from Panama and at that position of latitude the winds and currents should be favourable for a Pacific crossing. Only 700 miles *but* . . . and that was an awfully large but, because the current was against us all the time. The wind was against us too, when it blew, which meant that we had to beat into the wind, tacking back and forth like mad in order to make about 20 miles a day. On top of this the wind would, often as not, die out completely and we would drift slowly but surely backwards, carried by the currents over much of the distance that we had worked so hard to make. This was frustrating enough, but I haven't yet mentioned the rain, tropical rain that is, and tropical rain always seems at least three times wetter than any other sort.

Until now, my route had been that common to most yachts but now, perhaps because of the conditions I have just described, we found that very few yachts went this way. This made all the places we visited much more exciting because the locals were not used to seeing strangers come by water. Furthermore, the amount of land serviced by roads or tracks is almost nil along much of the coastline. Our first destination after leaving Panama was the Islas Perlas, a cluster of beautiful little green islands dotted around in the sea like small, sparkling gems.

As we neared the first island a hoard of native canoes—very small lightweight dugouts of much superior workmanship than those of the St Blas Indians—surrounded us, full of delicious fruit and big-eyed children. The fruit we bartered for and the children we tried to keep outside our boat, for they have extremely inquisitive fingers in this part of the world. We beached Shrimpy on a sandy patch to clean and paint her bottom (we had not touched this part of her in Panama because of all the muck in the harbour) but we had to work very slowly as the temperature was up to around 98 degrees. When this unpleasant chore was over, we continued wandering around these really pretty islands. I had to be on my toes, however, because we were again in tidal water (after the lazy almost tideless Caribbean) and it was very shallow in many of the bays.

After we left the Perlas isles, the sky clouded over and the weather got decidedly rough. We had to turn northwards and run with it in dangerously shallow water. Just before we reached the safety and shelter of a large estuary on the mainland, the wind died completely, leaving a very rough, confused sea, with a strong current pulling us towards a reef on which the waves were breaking horribly. All we could do was to try and anchor, so using the 100 feet of anchor chain plus all the rope I had on board (70 foot) we sat anchored in about 40 foot of water, bouncing up and down like mad with the front half of the boat at times diving completely under the water.

Suddenly, a line of breaking waves started to creep closer and closer towards us—the anchor was dragging! Luckily, a large fishing boat nearby spotted our predicament and steamed over to us just in time to offer us a tow out, before the breakers engulfed poor Shrimpy. I hastily accepted his offer but, sadly, despite immaculate seamanship of the fishing boat's Captain, the force of the sea was strong enough to demolish our pulpit and snap our samson post and leave three gaping holes in the foredeck, before we reached the comparatively calm and safe waters of the estuary.

Iris writes: 'When I started out on Shrimpy fear wasn't in my mind simply because of my ignorance of the sea, and every moment was beautiful. The time soon came when I learned to be frightened and to respect the power of the waves as Shrimpy got thrown about, joining the dance of the white horses, edging slowly but steadily towards the cliffs which were standing there like walls of death. There seemed no path leading beyond them.

'This exhilarating experience served to confirm my life's philosophy that it's better to *live* for one day than to exist for 100 years.'

When we were anchored the fishing boat came alongside—I thought he would demand a large salvage fee which he richly deserved—but instead he just wished us good luck and even offered us an extra mooring rope. A gesture which, judging from the state of his boat, he could obviously ill-afford. We were very moved by his kindness.

The next morning found me patching up the holes in the foredeck while Iris went to work sewing up the sails, which had ripped to pieces in that last blow. The terylene sails were now so rotted by the sun that they were forever tearing in anything more than a slight breeze, but we had lots of thread and a fair bit of patience. Just as we had finished the repairs, the rain began, the temperature plummeted and it poured and poured. We were quite cosy sitting in a calm anchorage inside the cabin, sipping tea and watching the rain, when we saw the shape of a huge dugout canoe slowly emerging from the gloom. Two men were in it without any protection from the rain and their gigantic outboard was obviously very sick. We invited them aboard, dried them out and filled them with hot soup and asked what they were doing out in weather like this. They explained that their outboard had been lame for some time but as they were, by profession, smugglers they had to pick their landing spots very carefully! After a few hours of warmth, they thanked us for our hospitality and continued on towards their secret destination.

By the next morning, we had Shrimpy in a sailable condition and we set off down the coast again and soon reached the snug anchorage of Pinas bay. The village here is cut out of the rain forest. All communication with this village is by sea and the jungle is so thick that there are not even paths, let alone roads. We had to anchor about three-quarters of a mile away from the beach because of the tremendous surf and were paddled ashore in the skilfully-handled canoes of the locals, which ride through the waves at frightening speeds. This bay is indeed a completely undiscovered surfers' paradise.

From here we continued along the coast, stopping now and then at little sandy bays and trading with the few Indians we met in this beautiful, sparsely inhabited, part of the world. We then reached Buenaventura, a God-forsaken little town which lies about ten miles up river from the sea on a muddy island surrounded by other equally muddy islands, covered with mangrove swamps and mosquitoes. The place is perpetually damp and any day with less than half an inch of rainfall is commented on as exceptional. Most of the people are extremely poor and the few rich ones have to employ armed guards who, by necessity, have to be expert marksmen to keep their jobs. We were perhaps the first yacht to pass through this dump without having anything stolen. This was mainly thanks to a group of young dropouts (?) on a motor yacht, who allowed us to tie alongside them and who kept watch on Shrimpy for us when we went ashore. They were amazingly cheerful and kind considering that they had been stuck there with engine trouble for two or three months already, and because of the appalling conditions, their boat was fast disintegrating under them. We just hope they managed to get away eventually.

From the hell of Buenaventura, we sailed straight into the paradise of Gorgona Island! This is a luxuriously vegetated extinct volcano about ten miles off the low, swampy mainland, with which it makes a pleasant contrast. It is also Columbia's prison for murderers! After all that I had heard of Latin American prisons, Gorgona Island was unbelievable. The head warden had been sent on a tour of European prisons and concluded that his establishment was more humane and more modern in its buildings and rehabilitation facilities than most in Europe. He was right. I would much rather spend ten years here than one year in Dartmoor.

We beached Shrimpy on the flat sandy shore at high tide, but I had forgotten that this was the highest high tide for two weeks, so we found ourselves well and truly neaped when the next tide failed to float us. We were a bit concerned about having to stay on this island for so long a time and wondered what kind of official trouble we would get into. We needn't have worried, however, for we were very well treated by warders and prisoners alike. The prisoners helped to repair the holes in Shrimpy and one of them, a tailor by trade, mended all the sails and strengthened them by cutting up our sailbags and sewing them in (there being no terylene material on the island). We were wined and dined at every meal time with wonderful food—so good was it that we called the dining room 'Gorgona Hilton' and secretly made a sign to that effect from varnished wood and with great ceremony, presented it just before we left. The prisoners gave us so much of their possessions and their hearts that it was almost painful and we left this strange island of enforced paradise with tears in our eyes.

After three more days of sailing we crossed the border between Columbia and Ecuador. The change in the type of coastline was abrupt; from jungle to—well, almost everything else. For the 500 miles of Ecuador's coastline has everything from desert to forest, from mangrove swamp to brilliant sand and the changes are so sudden that neither of us wanted to sleep for fear of missing some of its beauty. The first port in Ecuador that we came to was Esmeraldas, a pretty little town situated on the mouth of a shallow river. Here we met a customs officer who was so helpful and concerned for us that he did all our shopping, sorting out the bargains and making sure we weren't 'done'. Here we also met a tiny American tugboat with a crazy, beautiful crew aboard. They had towed a big, old drilling rig all the way down from the States and were beginning to believe all the people who told them they were mad to come so far in such a small tugboat, but when they saw little Shrimpy arrive, they knew they were saner than some people!

The next port we visited, a few miles further along the coast was Manta, a modern but still attractive town where there is a large fishing fleet. This fleet consists of about 200 dugout canoes about 20 feet long and 18 inches wide. Carrying enormous sails, they go 20 to 30 miles out from land chasing the big game fish—sailfish, marlin and shark. When they hook one of these monsters, the canoe gets towed along at impossible speeds for three or four hours until the fish tires. Then, at the end of the struggle, the fishermen have to sink their canoes in order to load the fish on board. After some frantic baling they then refloat both boats and fish and sail the 30 miles back to port—well, I suppose it's one way to earn a living.

From Manta we continued down the coast to Salinas at the mouth of the River Guyas. This town is the main seaside resort of Ecuador and sadly is a copy of all the bad features of US resorts and none of the good. Luckily, we had arrived in the 'off' season and most of the horrible skyscrapers were empty. Anchoring Shrimpy amid the many sleek, shiny game-fishing power boats in the calm sandy bay, Iris and I went ashore and spent the last few pennies we had on a bus ride to Guyaquil, the main port of Ecuador, which lies about 50 miles from the sea on the River Guyas. After collecting our mail from the main Post Office, we had a good look around the town. Now, completely broke, we faced a voyage across the Pacific. The next place we could hope to find work was Tahiti, 4,000 miles away! Somehow this town of Guyaquil must provide enough money, stores and repair material to get Shrimpy ready for the Pacific crossing. Unemployment here was great, neither of us could speak Spanish very well and, of course, it would be impossible to get work permits. Many strange thoughts went through my mind on the bus ride back to Salinas, but try as I might, I could see no way out. We were well and truly stuck.

Iris and I were in very high spirits despite our unusual situation when we arrived back on Shrimpy, for the sun was shining, the sea was warm and we were both used to living for the present. There was a party in full swing on an expensive powerboat anchored just in front of us and at a shouted invitation we went aboard and were asked to pay for our drinks by telling of our adventures. Happily, the three couples on board could all speak English very well and we soon became friends. Two of the men, Marco and Carlos, were very big in the Guayaquil Yacht Club and immediately offered Shrimpy free moorings for as long as we cared to stay at this very prestigious club in the heart of the city. They also invited us to visit their town houses after Shrimpy was safely moored in the club, so we decided to sail up the river on the very next day. The owner of the local charter fleet lent us charts of the 100-mile trip from Salinas to Guayaquil, pointing out all the dangerous parts of the estuary and river. He also quite unexpectedly gave us $50 and said, 'Pay me back when you reach Australia'.

Early next morning, we pulled up the anchor and set off on what was to be the most fantastic sail we had ever experienced. Everything was perfect, the wind, the sea and the scenery. We sped along the coast helped by the strong tidal current flowing into the estuary. As night fell we could pick up the twinkling lights of the buoys which led us into the mouth of this great swampy river and enabled us to reach the protection of a huge mud bank before we had to anchor for the six hours of ebb tide. As the tide raced out all night at over eight knots, Shrimpy sat on a very tight anchor chain quite comfortably, while Iris and I slept peacefully. Next day, the massive tide pushed us up river at incredible speed, almost too fast for us to drink in the beauty of the countryside, until we reached the town and could make out the pilings of the yacht club moorings. We had to anchor when abreast the yacht club and wait for the ten minutes of slack water before attempting to come alongside, for in this type of river you should really have an engine!

After Shrimpy was snugged into a mooring we were ushered into the club where a gourmet meal was waiting for us, provided by one of the members. While eating with this latest benefactor of ours, we learnt all about Guayaquil Yacht Club. Although it has good moorings for about 40 local pleasure boats, it is mainly a meeting place for the rich, with billiard rooms, card tables and one of the best restaurants in town. Furthermore, through the influence of our two recent friends, Marco and Carlos, the club committee had voted to allow us two poor yachties the run of the club and pick of the menu every day for as long as we stayed. We were at a loss for words.

Life began to take on a dream aspect; the red tape of South America that so many yachts have found so tedious and costly, melted away. Reporters from the five local newspapers made much of our adventures—one two-page spread comparing us with Ulysses! Then we were introduced to Chicken Palacios, a jovial, massive man who was the most famous sports critic in Ecuador. He took us on to his TV programme and actually demanded that the people of Guayaquil bring everything needed for our Pacific crossing down to Shrimpy. It came too; tins of food, paint, sailcloth, etc, etc. Carlos, Marco and their wives, one nicknamed the Cherry Queen for her love of, and staple diet of, cocktail cherries, took us exploring the countryside and game fishing—each time giving us a useful present such as a radio, binoculars, oilskins. On and on went this magical merry-go-round; wherever we went strangers smiled and wished us luck. It was quite embarrassing to accept all this generosity when all we had to give in exchange were our smiles. Iris with her gift for languages was soon speaking Spanish quite fluently, to the amazement of all our friends, while I struggled along, mainly with sign language.

In the midst of all this excitement another yacht—the only foreign one we saw in South America—sailed into the yacht club. This was *Christophe,* a French 30-footer, built in Paris but of the design of an Arab Dhow with modern-style rigging. We soon made friends with Jean and his wife, Maryse, and their small baby, Nicolas, who had been born while they were in Columbia and had spent more of his life aboard than ashore! We were to meet them again on the other side of the Pacific after they had a very hard time and, as Jean said, 'Sailing the Pacific is easy but sailing with a small baby—never again!'

Just before we were ready to leave, Iris became quite ill and doctors advised her that she needed at least one year's complete rest. Two people actually offered her the air fare back to Switzerland, so great was the generosity of these Ecuadorian people. Iris, however, had no intention of being a patient for a whole year and decided to continue with Shrimpy. I was not too concerned, having already discovered that her character and determination was such that no illness could hope to have an easy victory over her and, as it turned out, her recovery was complete.

We sailed from Guyaquil on December 10 1974, but left much of our hearts there. We drifted the 50 miles down the fast-flowing Guayas river to the sea in windless conditions and accompanied by local dugout canoes loaded to overflowing with bananas, balsa wood rafts floating down to the large cargo ships and the beautiful overrigged, engineless local trading yachts. Each time the tide changed we all had to anchor and sit watching the antics of the fishing pelicans and cormorants and try to avoid the sizzling rays of the sun which made the muddy mangrove swamps on each side of us shimmer and dance in the dazzling light.

After two days we managed to break free from the river and sail out across the steep, dangerously breaking seas of the bay to reach the long swells of the open ocean. Not without incident, however, for late one evening I was at the tiller when I saw a small, dull red light just ahead of me. Then while I reached for the torch I heard voices, then at the same instant as I flashed the torch, the lights of a large fishing vessel came on only yards away from us. The red lights I had originally seen were the cigarettes of the crew! It was a very near thing but we managed to miss each other somehow and continue on our separate ways.

We had only 500 miles to go to reach our next landfall—the Galapagos Islands, so we settled down to some beautiful days of sailing with the light winds and current pushing us nicely along. Shrimpy was looking good in her brand new colours, for the paint we had been given was white and red, so we had mixed it up into various shades of pink for different parts of the boat.

7

The Galapagos Islands and the Pacific crossing
December 24 1974–February 18 1975

Throughout the 12 days it took to reach the Galapagos Islands, the wind was so light and the sea so calm that I would willingly have made the trip by canoe. Finding nothing of interest on the radio, Iris and I spent much of the time singing to each other to pass away the days as Shrimpy sailed slower and slower in these light airs, for our mainsail by now was so patched and mis-shapen as to be very inefficient in these conditions. On the tenth day out we became completely becalmed about 100 miles away from the islands and were both lying in the cabin out of the sun. Suddenly a great roar—like the sound of a huge breaking wave—caused us both to rush out into the cockpit.

We were immediately enveloped in a fishy smelling mist and there, less than four yards away from little 18-foot Shrimpy, was at least 80 feet of blue whale, around 100 tons compared to Shrimpy's one and a half tons! Well, I've heard that these animals are peaceful and not to be feared but that did not stop me from being scared stiff, especially when this giant got curious and started circling around us, never more than ten yards away. We both stood staring, not daring to breathe or make any noise. Then, after a while he became tired of looking at us and for his farewell performance, he swam out about 100 yards in front of the boat then turned and came straight for us.

'This is the end', I thought, but just before he hit us he sank gracefully and passed inches below our keels and we never saw him again. (Since then we have had quite a few more whales doing the same thing but we're now becoming quite blasé about it.)

Two days after this incident we sighted the island of San Cristobal *dead ahead*. This quite surprised Iris, especially as it was the first time in her life that she had been out of sight of land. It quite surprised me as well—it always does! We had no permission of any kind to enter the Galapagos Islands as the Ecuadorian Government had stopped all yachts going there (officially that is) and even the combined influence of our friends Marco, Carlos, Chicken and even the Port Captain of Guayaquil had failed to remedy the situation. We had, however, been unofficially advised that the best island to stop at would be Santa Cruz, as the Port Captain there was reputed to be very humane. So, instead of stopping at San Cristobal, the main port, we spent three hard days of sailing—trying in strong adverse currents and almost non-existent winds, to make the Harbour of Academy Bay by Christmas Day.

About three o'clock on Christmas Eve, we gave up. It had taken us the last 12 hours to sail two miles because of the current and we had five miles left to go along the coast. Feeling very frustrated we anchored and Iris started to prepare a good meal to cheer us up. We couldn't even have a swim for there were at least 20 shark fins in sight, weaving all around Shrimpy. While we were sitting down to our meal we saw a local yacht chugging along the coast towards us. He threw us a line and without more ado, towed us into Academy Bay where, with great grins and shouts of 'Happy Christmas', he left us to anchor amid the three other (unofficial) visiting yachts.

We were rather apprehensive when an hour or so later the Port Captain came out to inspect our papers. We needn't have worried, however, for it was Christmas Eve, Shrimpy was the smallest yacht ever to have visited Academy Bay and all the local inhabitants, led by the famous ex-German, self-styled King of the islands Gus Ingenmeien and his brothers were all on our side. It would have taken a very hard character indeed to have refused us permission to stay, and the Port Captain was far from being a hard character. When we told him we had no papers he made a straight-faced throat slitting gesture then, with a huge grin, told us it would be OK. We stayed for four days in the beautiful clear calm waters of the bay, watching the fish clean Shrimpy's bottom and feeding the remarkable bold yellow warblers from our hands. These little birds were so unafraid that they would sit quite unperturbed beside you while you thrashed about to kill a fly then hop on your hand to eat the offering. It was also fun watching the outlandish dragon-like marine iguanas as they lumbered across the rocks or swam around the bay. We also visited the Darwin Research Station to see the famous giant tortoises clump around.

Gus, the King, was very happy that he could talk to Iris in German and showed us his 'cave' house where he lives, surrounded by whale bone furniture and decorations with the occasional stuffed shark and other weird and wonderful things. He also provided us with some of the scarce rain-water which he calls 'angels' tears' and saves for visiting yachts. The inhabitants of the island, by necessity, have become used to the very brackish local water which is unpleasant, if not downright poisonous, to a visitor. After a joyful, riotous Christmas party given by Gus, we left Academy Bay loaded with gifts of bananas, paw paws, butter and bread and sailed for Post Office Bay on Isle Floreana.

It took us three days of very difficult sailing to reach this anchorage, for the wind was still very light and the currents very strong in the wrong direction. When the wind died completely, instead of drifting backwards I tried the strange manoeuvre of attempting to anchor 15 miles out at sea in 75 fathoms (450 feet) of water! The first time, fearing that I might not be able to recover the anchor, I used the toilet tied to 100 fathoms of line. This didn't work, so over went the anchor! As the sea was so calm we had no problems and it saved us many hours of frustrating sailing and, sooner than could have been hoped, we arrived at Post Office Bay. This place became famous because the old outward bound whaling ships used to leave their mail here to be carried home by the first visiting homeward-bound ship. The letters were left in an old rum barrel at the head of the bay. All the visiting yachts in later years have continued this custom and each yacht has erected a small sign, with its name and date, near to the 'Post Office'. We discovered, much to our chagrin, that today the bay is invaded weekly by tourists flown out to 'do' the islands and has, of course, lost all of its magic.

Now, for a change of pace, I will take you on the longest leg of the voyage, 45 days across the vast, empty part of the Pacific Ocean, by using the words from my logbook, with additions, expansions and explanations in italics.

Iris writes: 'I knew that there were now 40 or 50 long days ahead of me, completely at the mercy of the sea, completely out of touch except for a small transistor radio to tell me if an atomic bomb had been dropped. It was a new feeling of insecurity which slowly changed into a new feeling of freedom. I was a bit frightened, not because of big seas, not because of sea monsters, but because the monotony of the surroundings did not provide enough change to keep my thoughts from going too deep. I had never had this type of experience before, there had always been an opportunity to change my path.

'As I found myself, for the first time, surrounded by water and sky, I felt so small—a nothing—and I couldn't believe how big and important I used to make some of my problems seem. There was the immense sea and there was I helpless in the grip of his force and power, I suddenly knew how gentle he was towards me; for compared to his size even a storm was just a playful game.

'My thoughts went around in circles, from the water to the sky, from sunrise to sunset, from childhood to age, from birth to death, from before life to afterlife, around and around; to become one, to end in one, to start in one.'

Day 1: Saturday January 4 1975
Set sail at 9.00 am for Marquesas, wind almost non-existent—Iris cooked a beautiful banana custard—made only about 20 miles by nightfall, but it was a pretty day as west we go into the sunset, *slowly.*
Day 2
Last night the wind was dead calm and the sea very bumpy—horrible. It

stayed calm until about 1100 hours then the wind gradually got up to Force 3 from south-south-west and we made some good headway. Had delicious maize in milk and egg for breakfast. No land in sight anymore.

Day 3

Wind almost died out last night and started again about 10.00 this morning but still only from south, still making slowish progress—chips for lunch—Iris remembered how I said I would not let anyone cross the Pacific with me. *Its amazing how things change isn't it?*

Day 4

Wind all day but not gone east of south at all yet. *The trade winds that we wanted blow almost constantly from the south-east or so say the pilot charts!* Had chips for lunch again and I tried to make batter fritters from flour and milk *with bananas* which turned out edible at least. Cloudy all day but not too cold.

Day 5

Woke up to quite good wind and another beautiful day, but the winds not good enough to be able to self-steer yet. Tried but failed to get a time-check, so decided to wait until tomorrow for our first sight fix since Galapagos. Started seeing flying fish again—almost the first we've seen in the Pacific.

Day 6

Got a time check last night and this morning I discovered that we had made good southing but only 250 miles actual distance from Post Office bay. Considering the wind conditions, that's not too bad. Iris made some beautifully chewy toffee.

Day 7

Mended automatic steering this morning and got it working tolerably well. Iris has had a bad headache for 24 hours now despite being dosed with pain-killers—maybe it's too many of these rough ciggies—*Ecuador's cheapest brand 'Full Speed'.* Will try and get running sail to steer for us tonight.

Day 8

Cloudy and drizzly day—not enough sun for a noon sight. Spent last night self-steering with the running sail, but slowly as the sail angle had to be so great to keep us on a correct course.

Day 9

Sights gave satisfactory progress—sunny day and fast sailing.

Day 10

Sunny day, very little cloud. Made pancakes out of the last of the bananas today and also some extremely good porridge with milk and cinnamon.

Day 11

We had a very rough, windy night and bumpy seas; the rough stuff is

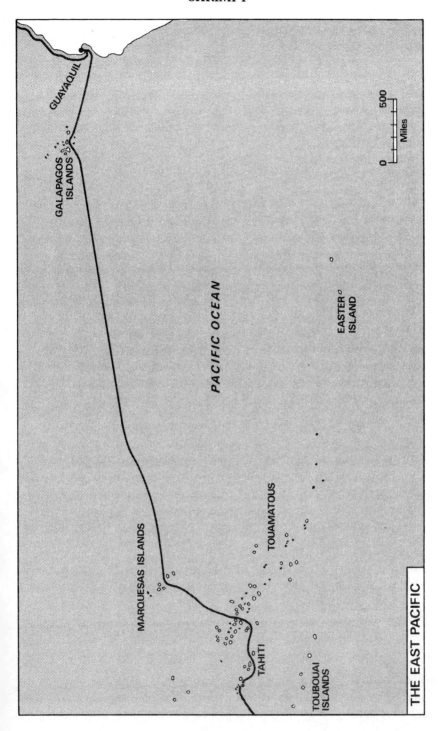

THE EAST PACIFIC

continuing today but we still seem to be making good progress without any sail up. The front of the cabin has started to leak again. *The leak was quite small but really annoying to Iris as it was her bunk that was affected.* Had to sew up mainsail which was badly ripped by the wind—a horrible job.

Day 12

Sailed with self-steering under the Genoa last night without having to give it any attention at all. *It is unusual for Shrimpy to self-steer under the big Genoa sail.* Extra large meal of potatoes, onions, beans and bacon tonight. Saw what looked like a pink fish fin. (Albino shark?)

Day 13

Had a big clean up of the boat today, everything getting a bit damp because of this annoying leak. Sights gave us a position of 800 miles from Post Office Bay.

Day 14

Wind changed back round to south. Had to take down running sail and put up the main—sailed quite fast all day. Had trouble with the Primus cooker, due to dirty paraffin. Picked up the BBC exceptionally well today on our little radio.

Day 15

Woke to find a snake mackerel or 'Gempylus' on our fishing line. We photographed it, then let it go as it is meant to be very rare. The *Kon Tiki* voyagers claimed to be the first people to see a live one—are we the second? Today was very bumpy and to top it all I had to take the Primus to bits again. *On reaching the Marquesas we discovered that every yacht crossing the Pacific had caught at least one 'Gempylus'.*

Day 16

Got running sail up again last night and all day today; going in the right direction but very slowly. Both lazed in bed all day, reading and listening to the radio.

Day 17

Lazy day again, nothing much happened. It has been cloudy and squally for three days now.

Day 18

Weather seems to be cheering up a bit and we are sailing along nicely. Opened one of our two tins of meat and cooked it with pasta and tomatoes—beautiful.

Day 19

No entry because the page is covered with a word game that Iris and I were playing.

Day 20

Slowly sailing along under the running sail. Glorious day. Have perfected our bread recipe—oats, flour, baking powder, milk. The result is better than shop bread. *Add a big pinch of salt to that!*

Day 21
Put mainsail up and steered all day to get a bit more speed; sea very calm and blue. Got Tahiti on the radio for the first time. The language and the songs sound beautiful. Can't wait to get there.

Day 22
Lazy day, sailing slowly; heard Wimbledon took Leeds to a draw away from home! *Yes, I am a soccer fan.*

Day 23
Half-way.

Day 24
Another lazy day; saw many flying fish. Put up main and steered for a while as we are a bit too far north and the wind direction of south-east is not helping any.

Day 25
Flying fish for breakfast; little wind all day; bouncing about horribly.

Day 26
Sailed by hand all day and made good progress. Iris made the bread today and it was better than mine!

Day 27
Ideal wind all day, sunshine very very hot. Maize, apple and custard was a great success—really loosening up our tummies! *But you don't have to 'run' far on Shrimpy.*

Day 28
Sights found us still too far north—amazing! Opened our last tin of meat; we were looking forward to is as the label showed luscious salami. The contents looked nothing like that but turned out to be quite tasty anyway.

Day 29
Put up the mainsail again to get some southing; sea very bumpy due to a complicated swell pattern; wind not so good.

Day 30
Two-thirds of the distance. Had a school of dolphins round us all day. Spent most of the day making and eating toffees. Actually got the radio working on all three channels for a while! *It would usually only work on short wave.* Tahiti sounds closer every day.

Day 31
Discovered that the thousands of goose barnacles on Shrimpy's hull had grown so long as seriously to hamper our speed. Went over the side with a knife to clean them off. While in the water, I got stung by a passing jellyfish. It hurt like hell for a while and I lost the use of my left arm for about 20 minutes. Had to sew up the mainsail again; it's getting really rotten now. Drank the last of the coffee.

Day 32
Woke to find the sea getting very big and the wind very strong and had

to take all the sails down. A very uncomfortable, wet day but things were better by evening and we could put up the running sail again before dark.

Day 33
Beautiful day, sailing well. Passed the three-quarters mark today.

Day 34
Saw lights of a ship last night. Wind has at last settled to easterly; just what we need. Had an enormous curry for supper.

Day 35
Lazy day, very hot, lots of tuna fish around but we can't catch any. Iris' 'sleepy cow' letter is now decorating the boat. *I will leave that last sentence to your imagination; hope you've got a good one.*

Day 36
Met a Japanese fishing boat today. They seemed very surprised to see us and circled us twice, with all the crew's cameras working overtime. One crew member got so excited that he forgot to remove his toothbrush from his mouth before aiming his camera and almost committed an awful type of *hara kiri!* Their ship looked tiny in the swells, God knows what we looked like. Rice, flour and milk all ran out today, not much left now.

Day 37
Beginning to wish we were there—not too far now.

Day 38
Entry too faded to read.

Day 39
Sea and wind very high, but we hung on to the sails and went very fast all day.

Day 40
Still going fast but wind has started to die.

Day 41 No entry

Day 42 No entry
I can't remember the reason, if any, for this.

Day 43
Hardly any wind. Sailed through a group of whales, one of which was standing head down in the water smacking his tail to and fro on the surface. It was an awesome sight and we wondered what it meant. By 10 am we saw land birds fishing and the sextant showed we were only 60 miles from shore. *1300 hours*—Sighted land! Isle of Ua Huka.

Day 44
Passed north of Ua Huka, a beautiful, rugged island; we saw no sign of habitation.

Day 45
Sailed into Taiohae Bay on the Island of Nuku Hiva—fantastic place.

*   *   *

Right *A view of Shrimpy's 'back garden' in Papeete harbour.*

Below *Suvarov, Tom Neale's lonely paradise.*

Below right *Tom Neale's house on Suvarov.*

The mighty Pacific begins to overwhelm Atiu harbour and its sole occupant Super Shrimp.

Above *Palmerston Island, a Pacific paradise.* **Below** *The end of a 'Red Tailed Tropic Bird' hunt.*

Above *The house we were given on Palmerston Island, '. . . for as long as you wish to stay'.*
Below *Searching the horizon for land. Australia must be out there somewhere!*

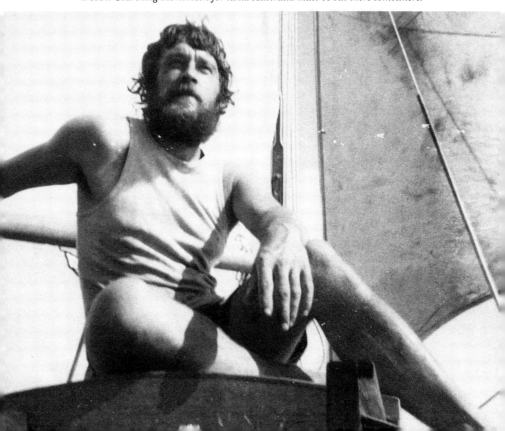

The last few days' entries in the above log do very little to describe our feelings when we knew that land was near. By about the fortieth day, we had run out of everything except oats, salt and water, and things began to get a bit hard. The fact that the cigarettes finished at the same time as the decent food did not help matters. We were both getting bored and considered we had spent enough time on the sea for a while and needed a rest.

When, on the forty-third day, we sighted the land birds our spirits rose for even knowing you are near land does not help mentally until you actually see some sign of it.

The moment we saw land was a very strange affair. For Iris, it was the same momentous experience that I had had sighting Barbados after the Atlantic crossing, but for me it held little more than any other day. Iris thought I was just trying to play the 'cool' Englishman—but that was not the case. Perhaps that is part of the reason why I am a wanderer—to seek new emotions, I need to seek new experiences. There are certainly many waiting just ahead because, at long last, Shrimpy had reached the first of the many South Sea Islands.

Iris writes: 'Searching the horizon for land—nothing but water—we could be near it, searching, a black dot, nothing—water—searching in the direction the seabirds are flying home, nothing, night is falling I can't sleep from excitement, the wind drops completely, I feel like screaming or pushing the boat, daytime, the same, over and over, black dot, no—water—a black dot, still a black dot, yes? Hm—no can't be, yet still there, fatamorgana—imagination—no! Still there! getting bigger, *land!!* It's land, it *is* land. Can I still walk? Suddenly I can't sit still any longer, let's jump up and down. Shane's playing it cool, I jump for him, I shout for him, *land!*

'Slowly the black point on the horizon begins to grow, from a dot into a smudge, I can't wait to get nearer, to discover its true shape, slowly we can make out the peaks of the mountains, the greyness changes into browns and greens, trees, bushes, grass, shadows in cracks of rocks, the sea-smoothed cliffs give way to craggier sculptures leading us into the bay. Smoke, houses, canoes, *people!* How I want to exchange words, how I want to embrace everybody, including the island, but water is still between us. Hello—waving hands—smiles. The first step on the sand, touching it with my hands, the island dances under my feet, it makes me dance with it. I am overwhelmed with happiness, the power of my joy is travelling on before me, catching all the people around me, travelling further, right to the last house in the village, encompassing the whole island, my whole world.'

LANDFALL

And when we finally reach the shore,
And when the sails are furled,
And when the boat's at rest again,
And earth is part of our world,

And when the bottom's scrubbed and clean,
And when the paint is new,
And everything's fresh water seen,
And bathed in morning dew.

Will you remember the endless swell,
The sting of the salt sea sprays?
Will you remember the singing wind,
Those forever lazy days?

Will you remember the whales we saw,
That filled us with awe and fear?
Will you remember the flying fish,
The dolphins that leapt so near?

Will you remember the birds that flew,
In that perfect summer sky?
And the little fishing boat we met,
Rusty, but proud and dry?

Will you remember our brave little boat
As she drove forever west?
Will you remember the songs we sang
And all the thoughts we expressed?

For if these visions stay in your mind,
And do not fade away,
The call of the sea will be in your blood,
Until your dying day.

Shane Acton
(Mid-Pacific)

8

Nuku Hiva and Tahiti

February 18–October 23 1975

Nuku Hiva is the main island in the Marquesas group and, as we sailed into the large natural amphitheatre of Taiohae Bay, we became enveloped in the sheer beauty of the South Seas. This place is thought of by many yachtsmen as the ultimate anchorage, with good reason. It has towering, barren, volcanic headlands of indescribable shapes like bricks piled haphazardly, as if by a child god at play, guarding the even more mountainous, but rich, green hinterland. Sandwiched between this at the head of a calm sandy bay, the pretty little village of Taiohae, 700 people strong and capital of the group, takes up all the flat land available.

We dropped anchor amid the three other yachts which were there and were immediately showered with gifts of fresh bread and fruits—the two things we had missed most during our 45-day Pacific crossing. We had already met one of the yachts in Galapagos and each of us was happy to see that the other had arrived safely. We soon made firm friends with the other two and also the many—50 or so—which arrived during our month's stay. Yes, 50 in a month, for this anchorage is a great crossroads of cruising yachts from all different nations, built in all different shapes, sizes and materials. Some shining new, others falling apart, and each one carrying exciting people—because people who cross the Pacific in small yachts are (whatever else) not dull!

Once ashore, our first impressions of this paradise were not at all dimmed by a close-up of the village. The five or six roads—all unpaved—are swept clean and watered every day. The small plywood and coconut leaf houses are surrounded by gardens of grapefruit trees, banana plants, breadfruit trees and many other goodies, all in amazing abundance. Everything is clean and airy and there are no fences to keep people away. The facilities include a hospital, post office, police station, bakery and three shops, also a football field, basket ball, handball and tennis courts and many small wall-less community huts.

The people are kind, generous and beautiful—especially the girls—but, sadly, have lost the art of tattooing which used to be common years ago. There are, in fact, no pure-blooded islanders left and the total population of the five villages on the island numbers only about 2,000, compared with the estimates of around 25,000 of the 'pre-discovery' days. They love to trade with passing yachts for things from the outside world—more for curiosity than gain—although .22 bullets used for hunting are as gold dust to the islanders.

The island's only income is from copra—the dried flesh of the coconut—which is used in the manufacture of margarine and various other foodstuffs. The average worker can make enough money from copra to live quite well despite the high prices of all imported goods. The most commonly eaten foods are fish (usually raw with lemon and coconut milk), beef (wild herds of cattle roam the interior), bread, breadfruit, rice and bananas. Many other fruits grow in abundance, so much so in fact, that a lot goes to waste.

Maurice is the local copra king and he also runs the best store on the island. He is very interested in all the yachts which arrive and keeps a book for visiting boats to sign. He told us that *Super Shrimp* was the smallest yacht ever to have visited the island and when he learned that we were broke and needed money to continue sailing, he gave me a job helping to load the trading schooner from Tahiti with his copra—collected by Land Rover, from all over the island—and to unload all the provisions, wood, cement, etc, which the boat had brought him. The job was great fun, but also very hard work as it was the first real manual labour I had done for two years and the temperature was always way above 80 degrees.

Out of the village, little tracks just wide enough for a car cling precariously to the sides of the mountains as they meander along to the outlying villages. Iris and I would wander upwards along these tracks, passing little plantations of bananas and coconut trees, situated wherever the way crossed a small cool stream. We would stop every so often to gasp in wonder at a new bit of scenery a bend in the road would give us. When we were high enough to find a cool breeze we would sit and gaze at the sea while eating a freshly picked mango or paw paw and, perhaps, drinking the cool refreshing milk of a young green coconut. As we got to know the locals better, we were able to discuss with them their problems and fears and discovered that this little paradise is not without its parasites. The lesser of these evils are the insects—mosquitoes and no-nos which can get a bit lively in the rainy season. By far the greater evils are the French Government and the Roman Catholic church, and the great shame is that this evil has such good intentions. For example, the Government supplies good schools and free education but also supplies French teachers who can't speak the local language and have no intention of learning it. They enforce French laws and taxes which the easy-going islanders can see no point in, as money need only be a luxury item were the islands properly governed. The Roman Catholic church demands that the people discard and forget all their 'heathen' history and culture and even goes so far as forcing European names on to the children before they are allowed to be baptised! Despite this, Nuku Hiva is still a fantastically beautiful island full of the friendliest people in the world. Perhaps, with luck, just isolated enough to avoid the hand of commercialism for many years to come.

But the grass is always greener . . . so onwards, Shrimpy, onwards. It's only about a week's sail to the atoll islands of the Tuamotu group.

★   ★   ★

The sun was shining in a clear blue sky, the light breeze was dead behind us and the sparkling warm sea breathed gently as Iris and I settled ourselves once more to the endless rhythm of the waves. But not for long this time, as we only had a mere 500 miles to the atoll of Takaroa, the most northerly of the Tuamotu Archipelago. This area is considered to be one of the most dangerous places in the world to navigate a sailing boat, as the atolls are no higher than sea level and largely treeless. Even where the trees are in abundance, you can only see the atolls from a distance of five miles. In addition, variable strong currents do their best to push you miles off course. The abrupt depths of large Pacific swell make it impossible for a small boat to anchor outside the lagoons; instead it is necessary to wait for the ingoing tide to sail through the narrow passes to the calm water inside. As the current runs up to ten knots and Shrimpy's speed is about four knots, this was often a very difficult exercise.

I gave every consideration to my little plastic sextant as we drew near to Takaroa and every five minutes Iris or I would climb on to the cabin top and scan the horizon. Amazingly, the island appeared exactly when and where it should have done, but as we neared the pass the wind died completely, giving us some agonising moments until a little motor boat offered us a tow to the jetty. Takaroa is one of the smaller atolls, about ten miles long and four miles wide and the island on which the village stands is 400 yards by 200 yards, inhabited by about 150 people, one car, one shop and four churches! My first thought as we tied up to the jetty in the calm, clear fish-stuffed waters of the lagoon, was to run to the shop and buy some cigarettes (we had run out the previous day and were gasping) but this idea was quickly shattered by the locals who grinningly informed us that the shopkeeper was a Mormon and, therefore, did not sell cigarettes, alcohol, coffee, tea, sweets nor any other of those nasty types of drugs! Help was at hand, however, when the chief arrived because he was—in his own words—only 'un petit Mormon' and stashed away quantities of cigarettes each time the monthly copra schooner arrived. He invited us to his house to give us cigarettes and a passport stamp. Although his house was only 40 yards away, he insisted we go by car, because he loved driving—so much so, in fact, that although there was only one car on the island and one road circling the island, there was a one-way system in force!

We were treated very well by these easy-going friendly people and learned that their life was simple yet enjoyable. Their food source, to the average visitor, seems almost non-existent and consists solely of fish and coconuts because no other food will grow on the atoll unless they import soil from Tahiti at exhorbitant prices—but this is hardly necessary as they know so many ways of preparing coconuts and seafood that the variety of meals seems endless.

Iris writes: 'I was visited by some young women, all dressed up in their Sunday clothes, who invited me to their church. My only dress showed a bit of neck but to me it looked perfect to visit church in. They took me first to their home where I was happily welcomed by the whole family, and after a refreshing drink, they led me to the women's room, and showed me some dresses from which I had to choose one. Proudly they explained how these garments had come all the way from the high priest of their religion in America, the dark colours and high necked pattern didn't appeal to me at all, I much preferred the local styles which were much more suitable for the climate and the girls, who looked as if they would soon suffocate in their new fashions. However, they insisted I dressed in one of those foreign frocks because it was not allowed to visit the church showing your neck; well my neck was covered and they didn't seem at all worried about my panties which were peeping out under the hem of the dress! Everybody satisfied, off we went to church, soon the singing started, children played hide and seek among the pews, while young lovers embraced each other in the back row. The sermon lasted too long for one woman who suddenly burst into song and everyone else quickly joined in, after this everyone joined in such a long gossip session that it was hard to believe that they all see each other at least 20 times a day. That same day I got two more invitations to visit two different churches, one had no more than three members—one priest, and a husband and wife.'

In the end we were driven from the island by the swarms and swarms of flies, for we had become so lazy that we were unable to put up with their constant buzzing and tickling. We sailed on to Apataki, a much larger atoll in the same group about 100 miles further south-west and stayed for a few days, but all the time there we felt an overwhelming desire to set sail, for we knew that less than 200 miles away was an island with a 'name'—a name which for many years had meant paradise as it called to me from Europe's libraries and travel agencies. The name was Tahiti.

As dawn broke and a blood red sun began to climb into another golden sky, I looked down over the bow of *Super Shrimp* as she rose to

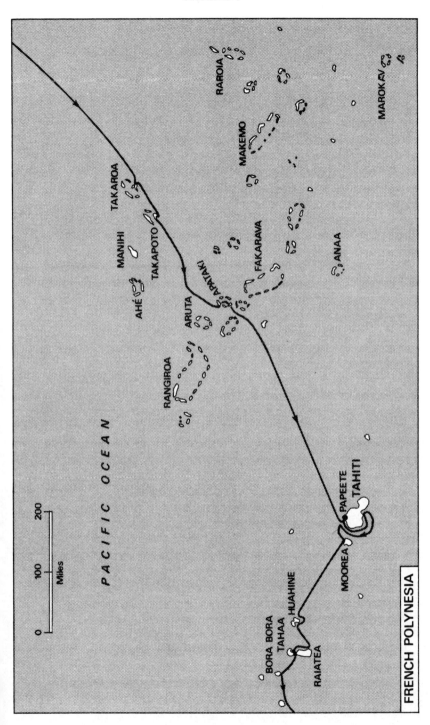

the crest of yet another giant Pacific swell, and there spread out before us glittering like an emerald was the island of which dreams are made—Tahiti. I woke Iris and together we watched the island grow as a fresh breeze pushed us quickly along. By 10.00 am we began to see in detail the velvet greens of palm and banana trees covering the towering mountains and deep valleys, and the occasional white line of a waterfall. Then, half a mile from shore, we met the breakers which mark the coral barrier reef which surrounds the island and leaves a calm channel of water between it and the coast. We sailed past Point Venus, where Captain Cook landed to observe the transit of Venus many years ago, and then through a gap in the reef that leads into the calm, clean harbour of the capital town—Papeete.

We tied up at the quay—which is right in the centre of town—and found ourselves amid many other adventurous yachts and yachtsmen, many of whom we had already met at various other ports throughout the oceans. Before we could fully relax, however, there were one or two problems to overcome. The first, as always, was to raise some money, for we had arrived with less than £1 at this, the second-most expensive town in the world. Already, we were in debt, as it costs £4 just to enter the harbour! The money problem soon vanished, for within two hours of arrival, I had found a job and was hard at work on a yacht called *Pai Nui*, getting it shipshape and ready for sea for its new American owner who employed all the poor 'yachties' for very generous wages. One workmate and friend in particular was an American shipwright called Richard, whom we had met previously in Nuku Hiva and were destined to meet in many ports ahead. He was sailing in a beautiful trimaran called *Peregrine* which he had built himself and sailed with loving care. So fast and hairy was his boat, however, that wherever we met him he had either just hit something or was just about to.

A few days later, Iris too was at work in the main Duty Free shop in town. She got the job mainly because of the fact that she speaks most European languages, but it turned out that the only tourists rich enough to spend money there were Japanese, so all she had to do was say 'Ah so' with a French-Tahitian accent! We were soon well-established and very happy, but it didn't stop there. Iris' boss had a two months holiday in France lined up and wanted someone to look after the house and pets. We jumped at the chance and were soon living in a luxury house with Shrimpy installed in its garden where I could do all the small jobs that needed doing without worrying about getting sawdust in the supper.

Idyllic days passed as we explored the island—which is so beautiful as soon as you leave the tourist route behind and get out of sight of the ice block hotels and their imported food and fads. We spent quite a few months in Tahiti and were very lucky what with 'our house' and our jobs, Shrimpy sparkling clean and freshly painted with another free consignment of International Yacht Paints and, on top of this, Rolex of Switzerland sent us one of their incredible chronometers, which was a wonderful present as my Mickey Mouse watch and Japanese transistor timing device had just about had it.

But, despite all this, despite numerous friends and fun times, we were now ready to sail again and as for Tahiti? Well, once it was a paradise, it is now a 'rich men only' paradise and soon will be a mess. Not so, however, the other island of French Polynesia. Lacking the 'tourist money' curse, they are beautiful in the extreme and, as we left Tahiti and sailed slowly through these islands, stopping at a different anchorage each night in calm clear lagoons each island gave us its own version of paradise: sleepy Moorea, coquettish Huahine, fierce Raiatea (the original Havaki or Hawaii), small dreamy Tahaa and scenically startling Bora Bora; we spent two months in these islands and could easily have spent a lifetime. The hurricane season was now fast approaching so we set off on the short ocean passage of about 700 miles to Rarotonga, main island of the Cook group, with the intention of staying there until the season was over.

9

Captain in the Cooks
October 23 1975–April 15 1976

We arrived at Avatiu port, Rarotonga, at the end of October—becoming the smallest yacht ever to sail from England to the Cook Islands. And what a miserable reception we got. Not, I hasten to add, from the people, who are some of the simplest, kindest and most generous in the world, but from the government—a family-run patriarchy headed by Sir Albert Henry. A big fat customs official told us that we would not be allowed to stay unless we produced $2,000 bond and had at least $60 a week in addition for living expenses (the average weekly wage was less than $20) and that foreigners who want to stay more than two weeks are not welcome unless they're very rich. The customs officer himself was very unhelpful! He seemed quite unmoved at the thought of sending an 18-foot boat out into the hurricane season. While our argument with the government was continuing, our spirits were nevertheless very high, for the islanders were showering us with fruit and gifts and showing a kind of awe-filled interest in the type of life Iris and I were living.

At this time too, yet another glorious event took place, for into the harbour and into our lives sailed *Toa Moana*. This is the New Zealand cargo ship that plys between New Zealand and the Cook Islands and has a crew mainly of Poms (British emigrants). Until now we had made many friends and received much help and advice from all types of big ships throughout the world but the 'Tow a Banana' as she is affectionately called, easily surpassed the lot. In the months to come, we used to look forward to the fortnightly arrival of this floating mother who washed us, fed us and partied us. From Captain to Cabin Boy, we thank you *Toa Moana*.

After many arguments with the government they decided to let us stay until after the hurricane season—this being easier and cheaper than to get rid of us, for I had refused to sail by tiny boat westwards at this time of year. So off I went to look around the island for work. The job I found? A government job—yes, as Captain of the *Ravakai*, the only inter-island government boat, a 60-foot fishing vessel with a crew of six which visits the small outer islands of the group, exporting politicians and importing fish and fruit. The reason I got the job was that, bar the skippers of the two commercial vessels, in direct competition with the government, and despite the fact that I had no papers at all, I was the only person on the island who could navigate well enough to get the boat from one place to the next!

The first thing we had to do now was to get Shrimpy out of the miserable unprotected harbour, so we put her on a nice grassy piece of land just across the road and lived on her there. We never found out who owned the land, but once a month two workmen came and cut the grass which had become our 'front lawn' and, what with public toilets and showers nearby, Shrimpy became a nice little house despite the regular flow of tourists who were very puzzled at this strongly built native 'hut'.

My job as skipper of the *Ravakai* was great fun and the crew were real characters. My bosun was an old sea dog named Hebrew Masters who knew everything and, although over 70 years old, worked twice as hard as anyone else and never seemed to need any sleep. My engineer was a Gilbertese islander and was always so happy and polite and so concerned about pleasing me that whenever I would ask him, a day before a trip was due, if the engine was working all right, he would always answer, 'First class, number one, skipper.' Even if he had the damn thing stripped right down—which was often—and we very rarely left on time because of this.

Each trip we made was great fun, but the most memorable was a special fishing trip to Suvarov atoll. Here, on this tiny speck of land 300 miles from Rarotonga lived one solitary man called Tom Neale. The book he wrote of his six years alone on the island *(An Island to Myself)* ends when he left, apparently for good in 1963 but the call of his solitary paradise was too great to ignore. He returned and, when visiting the island in 1976, he was still there.

Along with all our fishing paraphernalia we also had many small gifts and letters for Tom from the people of Rarotonga. We also had three great sacks of mail containing letters from all over the world. For, apart from the great curiosity felt about this loner, a postage franking from Suvarov is quite a collector's item. As Tom was 75 years old, everyone was wondering if we would find him alive, let alone fit and well, as we sailed from Rarotonga.

Approaching Suvarov, the weather deteriorated quite badly and we had difficulty in finding this little atoll with its tiny islets, the highest being only 80 feet from sea level to the top of the trees. My bosun, Hebrew, had been here many times before and his parents had actually worked on the island long ago, so he was able to give me expert advice about the reefs as we sailed through the wide entrance of the lagoon and dropped anchor about 100 yards away from Tom's personal islet. On the beach stood a small dinghy, shining whitely in the sand and, as we watched, a lithe figure appeared from under the palm trees jumped into the dinghy and set out towards us. Tom was alive and well! He sprang aboard the *Ravakai* to the accompaniment of many camera clicks and immediately asked us for a cigarette, explaining he had run out of tobacco three months ago. We offered him our best, a Benson and Hedges filter. He looked at it disdainfully, shrugged his shoulders and said, 'Well, that will have to do for now', bit off the filter and proceeded to smoke. Never before had I seen such a wiry, fit, bronzed, 75-year-old European with such a lively interest in world affairs and who had humorous, yet serious, disgust for warmongers, developers and advertisers. Despite many assurances, I had expected to find Tom changed in some way from the 'normal' by his solitary life, but this was not at all the case and he seemed much less lonely or hermit-like than many people I've met in the great cities of the world.

We stayed in the lagoon for a week's fishing, hampered by large numbers of small sharks, and also collected a lot of the huge coconut crabs that abound in Suvarov. In all this time, Tom was just like a good neighbour, neither pestering us nor rejecting us, but naturally making very sure we would not forget to take his mail when we left. Tom was getting treated quite badly by the Cook Islands' Government. They give him a salary of $50 a year for being Postmaster at Suvarov, then immediately took most of it back by taxing his gifts from overseas. They have also tried to persuade him to leave the place he loves so much and cannot understand when he very politely tells them to go to hell. When we bade him farewell his message to Rarotonga was, 'I'm good for another five years yet'—and the rest! I thought.

*   *   *

Rarotonga is only 20 miles in circumference and Iris and I got to know every road and track during our five months' stay. We made hundreds of friends and what impressed us most was the complete happiness of the children, so totally different from the sour, suburban kids of big European cities. Near the end of our stay, I gave one of the resident New Zealanders navigation lessons in exchange for an old Seagull outboard motor, which would be of great help to us around the numerous reefs of Tonga and Fiji. So, by the beginning of March 1976, we put Shrimpy back into the water and were ready to go.

Iris writes: 'During the time Shane was working on the *Ravakai* I lived with a local family; there were two children whose parents lived in Australia, two from the neighbouring island of Atutaki, and the youngest one came from the same island as Hinanou, who looked after them all. Hebrew, the 70-year-old head of the family and only wage earner, worked as bosun on the same boat as Shane. The whole family

SHRIMPY

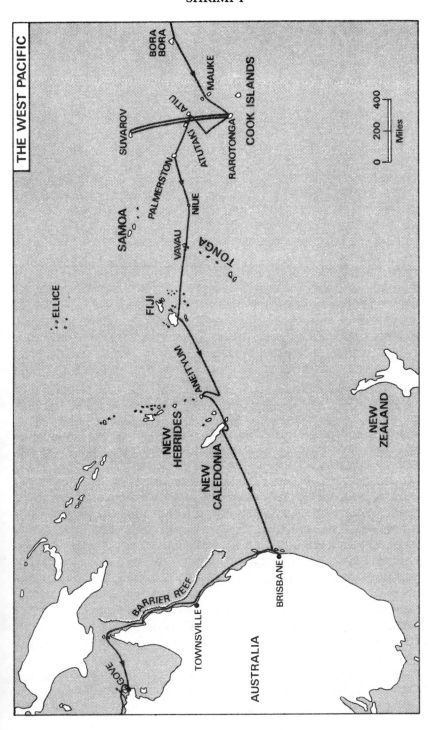

THE WEST PACIFIC

85

was a mixture of distant relatives living together, in fact everyone on the island seemed related in some way, and it was not unusual to hear a child call two or three different women 'mother'. Every one of the children had a different job to do in the home, Hinanou made sure they all did their allotted tasks, sitting under her mango tree giving out orders, chatting with her neighbours, getting fatter day by day, making sure the children were clean for school, making 'tiaras' out of flowers; then in the evening, lots of dancing and 'kung fu' movies. This was the way she spent her life. At night she would sleep at the front door of the hut on a bamboo mat spread out on the floor, to keep intruders from the girls who were near to courting age. The rest of the family slept together in one room curled up in blankets on the floor, when they were rich enough they would have an anti-mosquito coil burning beside them. I, the visitor slept in a separate room on the only bed, decorated with the most beautiful cushions and bedspreads, all made by Hinanou. When I left, the bed remained empty waiting for the next lucky visitor.'

*   *   *

We left the port of Avatiu and set course for Palmerston Island which I had visited previously while I was skippering the *Ravakai*. The trade winds had started up after the hurricane season and were blowing quite merrily—it was good to be at sea again. Our cheerfulness was soon dampened when, only six hours our of harbour, the wind stopped, then started blowing very strongly from the direction we wanted to go. The Pacific had decided to show us her power, a power which has no equal. We quickly had to down all sail as the wind rapidly increased in strength. The sea turned from its usually sparkling blue into a dull grey and the waves rose up and began to break right over the boat which was lying on its side from the sheer pressure of the wind on the mast. Then came the rain which turned day into night and night into hell as we drifted swiftly eastward, entirely at the mercy of the Pacific. For five days it lasted; five days of absolute misery in a dark damp heaving box of $\frac{3}{8}$inch plywood. We became very apprehensive and began to feel that it would never end. Then came a lull and, in the gloom, land appeared; a tiny island, surrounded by foam and dangerously near to us. A study of the chart showed me that this was probably Takutea and, therefore, the nearest inhabited land, Atiu, was about 12 miles away.

The lull turned into a prolonged calm but the currents were drifting us on to Takutea, of which the sailing directions state: 'Landing is difficult even in the best of conditions'. But *Super Shrimp* now had, for the first time since leaving England, another weapon in her very limited arsenal—the Seagull outboard. Having very little storage space the outboard had been lashed on deck and constantly soaked in seawater for the previous five days; if it didn't work now we would be on the reef—a last chance if there ever was one. Luck was with us and the ugly noise of the engine was sweet music to our ears. The calm continued as we travelled the short distance to Atiu island. Having been here before with the *Ravakai*, I knew the harbour well; I knew it had recently been built by the New Zealand Army; I knew it was too small for 50-foot *Ravakai* to enter; I knew it was only four feet deep at the entrance and I had a good idea that it would not be particularly safe in bad weather, but I didn't know just how bad it could get! Quite a large crowd gathered at the harbour at Shrimpy sailed in, for we were the very first yacht to do so and willing hands helped to secure the many ropes and anchors needed to keep the boat safely away from the walls. The slop caused by the sea breaking into the harbour was considerable, but Shrimpy looked safe.

For 12 hours all was well, but then the weather deteriorated again and the breakers began to swamp the harbour walls. We had to move, but it was impossible to leave the harbour—impasse! The only answer was to get Shrimpy up the ramp which led out of the harbour. Once again, the friendly islanders came to our aid and, in the pouring rain, men, women and children alike, heaved and tugged at the long nylon towrope. The shouts of excitement from the children each time Shrimpy moved upward, lightened the gloomy atmosphere and eventually, after quite a struggle, she was high, dry and safe! While waiting for the weather to abate, we stayed with the local '7th Day Adventist' preacher and his family and, although both Iris and I dislike the teachings of this religion, I must say that here, and subsequently in other places, these people have been extremely kind and what's more, genuinely helpful.

When the Pacific had calmed down after her tantrum, we lowered Shrimpy back into the harbour and the whole island turned out to wave goodbye and wish us good luck as we set off westwards once more. Because we had been pushed so far north-eastwards, we decided to sail to the island of Atutaki before going on to Palmerston Island. The sail to Atutaki was pleasant and uneventful until we were a few miles off the entrance to the pass. The wind was very light and I knew there would be a strong current in the pass so I decided to get the Seagull outboard set up and started before we got too near the reef. While I was prancing about on deck preparing all this, a sudden rogue swell caught me unawares and, in order to stay on the boat, I had to make a desperate lunge for the shroud. I missed it but it got wedged between my watch and my wrist. Luckily, despite the robustness of a Rolex wristband, my wrist was the stronger but our priceless gift—the chronometer which had made life so much easier—went spinning into the sea. (Later, in Australia, I wrote to Rolex to explain what had happened to their generous present and, to my astonishment, another chronometer arrived by return post with a letter wishing me luck for the rest of the voyage! What kindness—especially when you consider the fact that the price of the two watches together is more than I paid for my yacht!)

On top of all this, the Seagull had got so rusty that it refused to work, so we had to anchor outside the lagoon anyway. The next morning, we hailed a local fishing boat and were towed into the lagoon. As we made fast to the jetty we were very ready for a day of rest. This was not to be, for there stood the local representative of the Cook Islands' Government and a policeman. The policeman held a telegram which accused us of having stolen a whole load of radio parts from the main island before we left and orders to search our boat and make us leave the Cook Islands group immediately. This was obviously a face-saving ploy by the slob of an official who we had defeated by being allowed to stay on Rarotonga through the hurricane season. It made me see red, and I forced that poor policeman—who was nothing to do with it—to prod and poke through every single nook and cranny of Shrimpy which could hold even a single transistor let alone the gear on his telegram—the sum total of which would probably sink the boat. When this little charade was over and, of course, nothing found, the government official still insisted that we leave forthwith. I refused point blank and said first I needed a watch and, secondly I must fix the engine. To this she replied that if I didn't leave immediately we would be put in prison until I left. I explained that if this happened then I would never be able to repair the engine and, therefore, would never be able to leave. When faced with this type of situation, officials seem to lose all sense of logic so I ignored her and started work on the engine—after an hour or so she went away. We left two days later.

10

Small dots in the deep
April 15–July 31 1976

After a short pleasant sail we reached the atoll of Palmerston. Its several tiny islands are inhabited by one famous family—the Masters, about 20 of them—and, although the Cook Islands' Government appear to have some legal claim to the islands, the Masters consider themselves complete owners of their atoll. To Iris this was new territory, but I had visited them half a dozen times before as skipper of the *Ravakai* and had told them to expect us. As we approached we saw them launch their boats and shoot out through the pass to greet us. Soon we were in tow, for out motor was not strong enough to tackle the current in the small pass—so small, in fact, that hardly any of the usual size cruising yachts can enter—and then a short trip across the lagoon, dodging all the coral heads brought Shrimpy to rest on a blindingly white, sandy beach under the coconut trees.

We were then shown the house which was to be ours for as long as we wished to stay. Built from timbers of various shipwrecks, as was the church next door, this house had been used by many different people from Prince Philip to a group of shipwrecked Japanese fishermen. Here we rested in beautiful comfort while I told Iris what I had learnt about the Masters family.

Three or four generations ago, an Englishman—the first Masters—had been employed to develop the island's copra. His employer went bankrupt and so he comandeered the islands as payment and set up home. He got himself three girls from the Cook Islands as wives and lived a happy life. When he died, he divided each island into three parts—one for each wife and so the three sections of the family grew side by side. It is still that way today and, although there are only a handful of people to each section actually living on the island, they bicker quite a bit about the borderlines. (We had to be careful to make sure we divided our time equally amongst the three groups.) The entire family now numbers many hundreds and they are spread across the world, but any that decide to return to Palmerston are immediately given a share of their land.

Iris and I spent more than a week in these beautiful islands; everything was shared equally and we were included. We learned how to catch fish with coconut leaves, how to catch the wild booby birds, and many new ways to prepare meals of coconut. Each evening we would sit with the family and hear stories of shipwrecks on their coastline, of hurricanes that almost destroyed them, of Prince Philip's visit, of the single-handed yachtsman whose yacht they completely rebuilt after he was wrecked there, and many more. Eventually we decided we were ready to leave and, as we sailed out loaded with letters to post, kisses and gifts, a little bit more of our hearts was left behind us.

*   *   *

A few days of easy sailing further westwards across the Pacific saw our arrival at the second tiny 'country' an infinitesimal spot on the map—in fact non-existent on many maps—called Niue Island. A circular island of about five miles radius, 200 feet high and made entirely of coral. The main village, called Alofi, is situated on the western side of the island. Protected from the prevailing winds but not from the sea, is a small jetty and it is just off this that visiting yachts and ships anchor. The water is deep and the bottom very corally—precarious to say the least. Here also is the headquarters of Niue Yacht Club. The club consisted of one mooring buoy, one visitors' book and one yacht. These were the club's total material assets, but under the guidance of its founder— Peter Bailey—it produced one marvellous thing for visiting yachts, and that was hospitality unlimited! From the first fresh loaf of bread to the final hot bath, life ashore was one long party wherever we went—for the yacht club is the island and the island is the yacht club.

Niue, although covered with trees, has virtually no topsoil and the solid, razor-sharp coral rocks make farming very hazardous, so the main occupation of the happy-go-lucky islanders is producing children to send to New Zealand! For if you have about ten kids living and working in New Zealand and each one sending you a couple of dollars a week, life becomes very easy indeed. Fishing also provides great sport and the islanders go out to sea in their small dinghies and dugout canoes after enormous fish. The biggest one, after a two-day fight that carried a canoe and its two-man crew almost out of sight of land, had to be dragged up over the reef by bulldozer!

One kindly soul loaned Iris and me a motorcycle so that we could roam around the island tracks and visit the 13 or so small villages scattered across Niue. The fact that all the roads are unsealed and that I had not ridden a motorbike for about six years made my first attempts at getting the bike moving rather startling and put the fear of God into its owner. When all three of us (Iris, myself and the bike) returned safely and unscratched, the look of relief on his face was unbelievable.

On the third day of our stay at Niue, the wind swung around to the west, putting Shrimpy in a very dangerous position—anchored off a lee shore. Iris was ashore shopping at the time, while I was lazing on the boat. The swell got up so quickly that by the time she arrived at the jetty the waves were too big for me to get ashore and for Iris to get on board. The blow lasted right through the night and both Shrimpy and I were bouncing around like yo-yos. The waves at times broke right over the boat and the stretched anchor chain creaked and jerked ominously. At repeated intervals throughout the night, the disc jockey on the local radio station assured me that Iris had been given a nice soft, warm, dry bed and wished me a peaceful night! Luckily the anchor held until the wind turned back to its usual direction and the sea calmed down once more, but unluckily it held too well for, when we were preparing to leave a few days later, we couldn't get it up. That was a small price to pay, however, for our visit to Niue—the tiny island with a big heart.

Westwards, Shrimpy, westwards and after a few days of light breezes and calm seas, we could distinguish the islands of the Kingdom of Tonga dotted across the horizon—a thin chain of glittering emeralds in the clear blue sea. We had heard that the southern-most islands of this group, including the capital of Nuku'alofa, were very flat and very crowded, so we sailed northwards. Va'vau is the name of the northern-most group and it provides perhaps the best coastal sailing waters of all the Pacific islands. With calm clear sea, hot sun and cooling trade winds, yachts of any draught can safely sail in and out of the 50 or so islands which vary from sandy atolls to craggy rocks. The largest island, with its perfect 'hurricane hole' anchorage and main town of Neiafu, has one or two roads but the rest just have little footpaths weaving through the bush from village to tiny village, most of which have their own little sandy bay and a small jetty. Dugouts, dinghies and little boats of bent tin—nearly all powered by British Seagull—converge on Neiafu every Saturday in droves, carrying precarious loads of people and produce to market—where the prices of local foodstuffs are unbelievably low. Iris and I were soon on a diet of taro, yam, pumpkins, clams, bananas, coconuts, sweet potatoes and breadfruit—starchy but delicious.

Sailing around these islands we met many yachts already known to us from the Pacific route; notably Jean and Maryse on their beautiful dhow *Christophe* with baby Nicolas, who we first met as a babe in arms and have watched him grow from port to port. By now he had learnt his first words—'Mama', 'Papa', 'Zodiac', 'Poisson', etc. Anchored very near *Christophe*, we had an interesting day watching Jean bartering for native goods which the dugouts ferried around the yachts. At first they just offered him the usual small trinkets, but finding him a good customer with a large yacht, the size of the articles gradually increases until, at the end of the day, we watched with amazement as a carved tiki about the size of a telegraph pole was hoisted aboard *Christophe* leaving in its wake many upturned dugouts and grinning spluttering natives.

Another real character we met was Harry, a Canadian single-hander who had built himself a beautiful pea green coloured yacht. Only 30 feet long, it was so heavily and strongly made that it could probably win an argument with a large tanker. The only trouble was that being so heavy it was ridiculously hard to sail, so Harry spent all his time trying to make it easier. The deck had become a mass of rope, wire, block and tackles, but as he proudly demonstrated he could now pull the mainsail up with only one hand even while sitting on top of it—the sail that is.

One day a strange but beautiful looking yacht sailed in and, as we watched, none of us gossiping yachties could figure out what on earth it could be. Then its crew, a family of four, looking happier than anyone has a right to, rowed over and explained things. We were looking at the first 'energy crisis' fishing boat! A remarkable story followed. This English farmer, fed up with scraping a living from English soil, sold his farm and took his family off to New Zealand. There he persuaded the government to give him a grant to produce an 'energy crisis' fishing boat. I don't know if the plans got a bit bent along the way, but the finished article looks exactly like a luxurious sailboat with an extra-large ice box! So now this enterprising family spend their time 'testing' the marvelous new invention around the idyllic Pacific islands.

Back ashore the inhabitants of Tonga—the 'Friendly Isles' are friendly yes, but nothing like as happy and open as the people in other Pacific island groups we have visited. A very strange atmosphere exists and this, I feel, is due to three main reasons which together make a deadly melange: poverty, overcrowding and fanatical religion. The worst of these three factors is the overcrowding. Every bit of island is owned and used and we were severely reprimanded for gathering old coconut husks and other flotsam along the high tide mark to make a fire as it 'belonged' to someone. The road ahead looks very tough indeed for Tonga but I hope they can find a way, for theirs is a land of refuge from the cold old world.

As we set sail from Va'vau we passed two large tourist liners which were about to enter the harbour and we wondered if there was enough room on the island for all the passengers at one time or whether they would have to go ashore in relays!

About 50 miles west of the main Tongan group is Late Island which, for some reason, is completely uninhabited despite the overcrowding on the rest of the islands. It is a beautiful looking shape—pure textbook volcano rising many hundreds of feet and covered with vegetation. We sailed closely along its northern shore, but were afraid to land as the sea was quite rough and there would be no one to help us if Shrimpy went missing while we were away. So, leaving Late Island to sink slowly into the sea we headed west once more, bound for the islands of Fiji.

11

Up a river
July 31–October 6 1976

The islands of Fiji are scattered over quite a large area of ocean and they are protected on their eastern side by a long line of reefs at many points out of sight of any land. To avoid these reefs completely means a long detour to the south or north and to find one of the passages through them requires pinpoint accuracy with a sextant after many miles of vague currents and open sea.

As the weather was good, and by now I was feeling quite confident with my navigation, we decided to try and find one of the smallest passages, mainly because it was *The Bounty*'s passage—through which Captain Bligh had passed on his epic open boat voyage, after having been cast adrift from his ship *The Bounty* by his mutinous crew. Amazingly, we found it quite easily and steered Shrimpy through with giant rollers crashing on the reef each side of us and it was easy to see how a small boat could be lost there without trace, if it was unfortunate enough to hit such a formidable barrier.

A bit later we were within sight of the first outlying islands of Fiji, so it would be easy to avoid the many coral patches by taking compass bearings of the islands, or so I thought. But horror of horrors, the weather suddenly deteriorated until it was blowing a full gale. Huge steep seas, pouring dense rain and too much wind for the smallest sail! We just had to let Shrimpy drift around for a whole day in these coral infested waters, completely at the mercy of the winds.

This was perhaps one of the worst gales that we experienced through the whole trip, or perhaps it only seemed so bad because we were surrounded by those deadly coral patches which sit just below sea level. Even a large yacht needs a bit of luck in these circumstances, for even if it can still sail or motor on a set course, there is no way of knowing how much the wind and current are affecting the direction steered, and the breaking waves on the coral cannot be distinguished from the general mass of white seas.

All we could do was lie in our bunks, trying to get as much rest as possible, mentally as well as physically, for in such a situation the noise is appalling; torrential rain drumming continually on the deck, the regular crashing of each rolling crest as it speeds towards the yacht, then the thump as the boat is hit and engulfed by boiling surf. Next comes a hissing sound as Shrimpy is pushed along sidewards in the foam, then a few seconds of comparative calm as the next wave gets ready to fling itself against the fragile hull. If you've ever tried to go to sleep on the 'big dipper' at the fairground in a cloud burst you'll have some idea of what it's like—but that ride only lasts for a few minutes! The most frightening aspect of all is that you are constantly wondering how much worse conditions are going to get before they begin to improve, and how much more you can take of the continual noise and battering before you lose your sanity. You feel you would give anything just to have the boat stop lurching for five or ten seconds. You know, logically, that the gale can't last forever, but the more tired you get the less logical your mind becomes. Eventually you are sufficiently numb to come to terms with the fact that you must just sit and wait it out, for there is absolutely nothing you can do.

As the gale began to die down a bit and the visibility improved, I managed to make out the dim shape of a small island, then another; hurriedly working out our position I discovered we were about one mile to windward of a huge unseen reef! So we hoisted a very small jib and went careering along beam on to the seas until we managed to reach the safety of Totoya just before dark. This horseshoe-shaped island has an accompanying reef in the shape of an inverted horseshoe, making a perfect anchorage in any weather and we were very happy to drop anchor in the calm lagoon just as the hazy sun drooped tiredly into the sea. We stayed safe and snug in this anchorage until the gale blew itself out and then set off for the main island—Viti Levu—and reached the safety of the harbour with no further mishap.

It was about midnight as we entered the harbour and on the way in we were passed by a very big yacht who asked us where he should anchor and where the yacht club was. I replied that I couldn't help him as Shrimpy was a stranger here too. He refused to believe that tiny Shrimpy could be anything but a local boat and got very agitated that I would not tell him where to go—I was tempted . . .

Next morning found us sitting at anchor off the yacht club with our yellow quarantine flying, awaiting customs clearance when a huge million dollar New Zealand yacht arrived. After bouncing off a few other yachts and about three attempts at anchoring, they ended up very close to us. We were invited aboard for a drink and were dismayed to find ourselves face to face with a problem all too common on yachts. The Captain and crew had set sail from New Zealand on the maiden voyage of this luxurious craft which had just about every known electronic gadget on board for comfort and ease of sailing, but as time went on personality problems loomed large. Before we left Fiji, the beautiful boat had been left sitting empty in the harbour, its disenchanted Captain and crew having all flown back to New Zealand by different planes!

After sampling the cold, unhelpfulness of the Fiji Yacht Club, we quickly sailed across the bay to the anchorage off the Tradewinds Hotel, who give visiting yachts a much better deal at next to no cost, because this is the rainy side of the island and tourists stuck in their hotel rooms can at least amuse themselves by looking at all the pretty boats. An enterprising reporter living in the bay on a houseboat even managed to get himself, Iris and me a sumptuous meal at the hotel in exchange for including it in the picture he took of Shrimpy for the local newspaper.

Bustling Suva town—the capital of Fiji—seemed quite large to Iris and myself as it had things like traffic lights and lifts which we had not seen for a long time and to walk along its streets gave us both a claustrophobic feeling. Suva is, however, a very pretty little town and is pervaded by the delicious smell of drying copra. The strange thing about Fiji is that there are more Indians here than Fijians. The Indians were originally imported to work in the sugar cane fields, as the Fijians were much too lazy. Third or fourth generation Indians naturally regard Fiji as their home country and there is quite a racial problem. Indians have become completely dominant in the business side of life while the Fijians try to hang on to the government. They also hang on to the land and the Indians are banned by law from buying any. There did not seem to be too much friction on the surface, however, and the saris of the Indians mingling with the brightly patterned 'wrap-around' type skirts of the Fijians (men and women) make a fantastic display of colour

*   *   *

From the chart, I noticed that a large river—the Rewa—almost cuts the island of Viti Leva in two, so Iris and I decided to see how far we could get Shrimpy up this river and, at the same time, get to see some of the interior of the island. Having sold our outboard to get enough money to enable us to reach Australia, we asked if we could borrow it back for a few days! In return we invited the people who had bought it to come on the river trip with us. They were Vera and Larry, an American couple, whom we had met before in other islands and who owned and were sailing in the beautiful yacht Onza. They accepted the invitation and seemed to enjoy themselves despite Shrimpy's size and lack of luxuries that they were accustomed to. The estuary of the river, although muddy and shallow, had a well-marked channel but as we proceeded above the commercially used section, there were no markers at all and life became difficult. In places Shrimpy's slight draught was almost too much although the river was still half a mile wide. As the fairytale scenery floated slowly passed us, each bend would bring a new little village into sight and the whole population would run down to the river's edge. Even the schools were emptied and everyone stood and stared at Shrimpy—the first ocean-going yacht capable of ascending the river!

Our first major problem was a bridge which looked a little bit lower than the top of the mast. I approached it very slowly stern-on, ready to power away if I heard any scraping sounds, but we just got under. Further up our audience increased; everyone laughing, shouting, and waving. The experienced canoeists among them shouted advice as to where the deepest channel was. About 30 miles up river we started hitting the bottom so often that I became concerned for Shrimpy's safety. We decided to stop for the night and begin down river the next morning. The chief of the nearest village, a very interesting man, invited us to a party that evening and we willingly accepted. Presents in hand and all dressed up, we climbed a 50-foot cliff of oozing mud to reach the chief's cluster of woven bamboo huts. Here we were introduced to his sons, numbering 12 and the rest of his closest relations, about 40 in all. After the family had acknowledged our presents by clapping their hands—an old Fiji custom—we sat down on the bamboo mats and began to attack the feast which was laid out before us on fresh, green banana leaves: chicken, river fish, eels, taro, rice, breadfruit, coconut cream and tea. Then, as the table was cleared and the guitars started to play the haunting island songs, guests from other hamlets poured in, each one bringing a present—no matter how simple—and being courteously applauded. Eventually the party was in full swing and the ceremony of 'kava' began.

Kava is the local booze, but tastes very different from alcoholic drinks. Its preparation and presentation has quite a ceremony attached to it and in this family the ceremonial bowl was, unbelievably, a perspex observation dome which had been inverted and placed on a wooden frame! The kava is brewed on the spot in this dome, allowed to stand for ten minutes and then distributed in half coconut shells. The timing of your first bowlfull is up to you but once you have started the decision is out of your hands. When the bowl is presented to you, you must clap your hands first, drink the lot in one gulp and then you and everyone else claps and you say 'bula'—which seems to mean a combination of good morning, goody-goody and cheers. This whole routine gets more and more difficult with each drink you have! By two in the morning we were really ready for bed.

On our return to Suva, everyone in town recognised us for Shrimpy had made front-page news as the smallest boat to sail from England to Suva and we received many wishes of good luck as we prepared for the next leg of the voyage. Shrimpy was now more than half-way around the world—we were homeward bound!

*   *   *

When we left Fiji, Iris and I knew that if we reached our next port safely we would have travelled further around the world than any yacht of comparable size or smaller. For on arrival in Noumea, New Caledonia, we would surpass the record of *Sea Egg* which was unfortunately lost without trace off New Zealand. Well, we made it but not without a struggle.

The mere 600-mile trip was probably the most frustrating sailing we have ever experienced. The weather chart for this area at this time of year shows 70 per cent east or south-east winds and only 1 per cent west wind, but we found quite the reverse, plus a large number of calms and squalls, all of which forced us to sail all over the ocean and rarely in the right direction. After two weeks we were fed up with trying to sail into the wind all the time and turned northwards towards the island of Aneityum—the southernmost island of the New Hebrides group. Eventually, late one evening, we were within one mile of Aneityum, before the wind died for the umpteenth time. By next morning we discovered that the current had drifted us back out of sight of land and it took us all day to get anywhere near it again, but then the wind died . . .

This appalling state of affairs carried on for three days until, at our third attempt to reach the bay, we spied another sail approaching and eventually the yacht *Manuia* from New Zealand was near enough to chat to. Soon Shrimpy was under tow as *Manuia* gently chugged into port. Aneityum's harbour must be one of the prettiest in the world and the 300 inhabitants of the island are some of the gentlest, shyest, happiest of all people. There was one European on the island, a very eccentric fellow who runs a sawmill which is the only industry there. He rowed a little dinghy out to us as soon as we were anchored and commenced to play the role of stern official until he discovered that *Manuia* had lots of cold beer aboard. After a couple of cans we had a new friend and the freedom of the island. The place had one old bulldozer which was held together solely by vines and vigilance and it went off into the jungle each day, rattling like a busy dining room, to return each evening dragging a huge tree behind it down to the sawpit. Its return was a wonderful sight, for it was always festooned with flowers which its five-man crew had picked and was followed by a flock of birds who fed off the insects its weary tracks dug up. Somehow this rusty hunk of noisy metal was transformed into part of the incredibly beautiful scenery.

We left Aneityum when the good weather and favourable winds returned and soon we could see the high mountain ranges of New Caledonia. Then came a tricky bit of navigation through the reefs which stretched up to 40 miles off the coast to reach the main port of Noumea. We found nothing impressive about New Caledonia or its people but it must be nicer further away from the big, expensive town. The huge marina complex—while giving us all the comforts of home—left us cold and forced us to the conclusion that the mighty Pacific Ocean had almost been crossed and that Shrimpy's next resting place would be Australia. It was with a bitter sweet thought that we set sail from Noumea. We had sailed further than any other yacht of Shrimpy's size, but we were leaving the Pacific behind.

★　　　★　　　★

For the last leg of our trip across this mighty ocean, the Pacific showed us her most gentle face; soft trade winds quietly pushing us through the clean blue, sparkling sea beneath a sky of tiny white fluffy clouds and a warm bright sun. Fish allowed themselves to be caught with ease and life was good. Just before sighting land we had our last Pacific encounter with whales. This time, two large ones and a little baby bouncing merrily across the sea. It was a bit scary as the inquisitive baby headed towards Shrimpy as soon as he saw her and we were worried what his parents might do but, as always, no attack came and when they swam off we were left with the feeling of relief yet sorrow—that strange mixture of emotions that is so much a part of life on the sea. A few hours later, a little fleet of fishing boats passed us; land could not be far away now.

12

Brisbane the bountiful
October 6 1976–April 20 1977

The coast of Australia was just visible as the night closed in on us. The fact that we had no proper charts, just a sketch map, and that the coast is littered with islands and dangerous sandbars, dictated that we took the main channel route to the Brisbane river. This route is well marked by lights, but wiggles about so much that we had to steer all night. As dawn slowly lightened the sky, we could see the entrance to the Brisbane river before us. The water had become a dirty brown and was full of most revolting looking blue jellyfish which infest this area. We passed oil refineries, large tankers and busy tugs as we sailed up river towards the glistening towerblocks of the city of Brisbane—all the time wondering if 'Nobby' had managed to arrange anything for us. Nobby, or C.E. Clark to give him his proper name, was the man who had built Shrimpy in the Isle of Wight, England, many years ago. In fact, he had built hundreds of 'Caprice' Class yachts—of which Shrimpy is one—and had first heard of our adventures through the 'Caprice Owners Association' bulletin. We had been in touch with each other by mail for quite a while as Nobby was naturally very interested in the wanderings of one of his tiny yachts. In our last letter to him, we had asked if he could try and dig up a bit of publicity for us—as we would be the smallest yacht to have sailed from England to Australia—in the hope that we could convert this into some cash. Little did we know what waves we had caused.

Before we got anywhere near the city we were hailed by loudspeaker from the customs post on the bank of the river and asked to come alongside their jetty for clearance. They must have been watching our progress for quite some time, as they were well prepared when we arrived. There was a message for me to telephone Nobby, a hot bath for Iris, and a bag of fresh milk, bread, cheese and fruit! (Would that all customs officers were as thoughtful and kind.)

On the phone Nobby told me that arrangements had been made for a mooring at Manly Yacht Harbour and a boat was on its way to give me a tow through the backwaters and that he—Nobby—would meet me there. Customs formalities completed, we returned to Shrimpy. There was the tow boat waiting for us but also about a dozen little power boats full of Press reporters, TV cameras and anxious interviewers! There was even one reporter—Phil Hammond—from my local Cambridge paper back in England.

We were overwhelmed but didn't have time to catch our breath because the skipper of the towing boat explained that the tides demanded we leave immediately in order to reach Manly. So off we went at a speed unusual for Shrimpy, conducting interviews 'en route'. The Press boats, fighting amongst themselves to get alongside us made me quite anxious for Shrimpy's safety and the interviewers got their material at great cost—as we left behind a wake of bits and pieces of microphones, electric cable and TV cameras!

By the time we tied up at Manly, our accompanying fleet had become quite large and there, in the boat at its head sat a very proud, very happy Nobby!

Once more on solid ground, the Press regained their confidence and went to town on us for a few hours, but after a while it all died down and we were able to invite Nobby aboard for a chat. He introduced us to Vic, a friend of his who was arranging the publicity for us. He also explained that he lived in a small village 20 miles along the coast and that in a few days we could tow Shrimpy there and stay with him for a while—what a welcome!

The next morning Iris and I went off to see the immigration officials who managed to dampen our spirits by telling us that although I could stay a year—provided I did not work—Iris could only stay for seven days because she was Swiss and had no visa. Despite our protestations that we had arrived on a very much unassisted passage and that our method of arrival must prove that we had some degree of willpower and ability, it seemed that they would rather pay out-of-work unionised agitators to come from England to work for them. Realising this was just officialdom and not the way 'real' Aussies think, I called a Press conference (we were still 'news'). While explaining our position to them an official of the yacht harbour came up and told us we must move Shrimpy out of port the next day. Needless to say, the newspapers had a field day on their front pages and, as a direct result of this, offers of aid poured in from hundreds of generous Aussies and the public pressure forced the government to give us permission to stay and work in Australia for a year or so. (The permission was 'officially' unofficial for, although we stayed in Australia for a year and a half, they refused to record the fact in our passports!) The Port Captain personally came to tell us we were welcome to stay in his harbour as long as we wanted.

Iris writes: 'I was looking forward to 'big city' life, theatres, cinemas, the latest books, music, etc, were all ready and waiting for me to enjoy. But what a complicated way to get there, all the papers you have to sign, buying maps to find your way through the maze of offices, just to say

'I'm here'. More than this, you become a number rather than a name, all this trouble merely because you come from a different country wanting to see a few sights and meet a few people.

'It had become so natural to live the so called 'primitive life' of the Pacific islands that the reality of my European style 'civilisation' started to look very ridiculous; the press of the crowds in the street all rushing around, not smiling, not even seeing each other, no time for a chat, only elbowing and pushing to be first, first for what? It seemed to me that they themselves didn't know what they were doing, as if a big hand covered the city, with many strings hanging down, attached to and controlling all the people, making them dance like marionettes. How strange a pram now looked to me; the baby being constantly pushed away from the mother, make-up on faces to hide even their own masks, no crippled people to be seen, no room for their wheelchairs in the crowd anyway. All so different from the life I had become accustomed to in the past few years.

'Now the two worlds started melting together in my mind, the bright and dark sides of each, the softness and harshness of life in each, the images of each criss-crossing one another, to leave my mind confused, my thoughts chaotic. It became very difficult and frightening, my whole being was fighting to find some order. But I knew I would win the fight because all the beauty and love that I had seen and been given on the voyage, had provided me with a lot of strength, and deep down inside, a light that would never go out.'

A few days later a friend of Nobby's arrived in a little tin motor-boat, ready to tow us through the maze of backwaters to Woongoolba where Nobby lived and earned his bread running his own company—Woongoolba Marine. On arrival we put Shrimpy on a trailer, moved her into Woongoolba Marine's service yard and were soon installed in Nobby's house which was right next door. Here we met Hazel, his wife, and their sons Leslie and Raymond and soon felt part of the family.

During this time, Vic, our publicity man, had been quite busy and had arranged for Shrimpy to be exhibited around the various huge indoor shopping centres of Brisbane—who were willing to pay substantial sums of money. The next month or so had us following a very new routine; we would trail Shrimpy to a shopping centre, install her in the middle of the floor, erect the mast and sails (often having to make a hole in the ceiling) and for the next week we would pass the centre's opening hours sitting on Shrimpy with silly fixed grins on our faces, signing autographs and being 'interviewed' by Vic every couple of hours. The complex owners thought it a great success, but not so Iris, who got really cheesed off with the amount of ridiculous questions asked about her life at sea by very un-nautical-minded housewives such as 'What make-up do you use in a storm?' and 'How do you manage without a vacuum cleaner?' The thing that maddened me was that, as most ignorant 'experts' will kick the tyre of a car, so will they tap the hull of a yacht—and Shrimpy received any number of blows and thumps throughout her employment as an 'exhibit'.

On the happier side, this exhibiting brought us many invitations to give 'after dinner' talks of our adventures at various clubs and societies and gave us the chance to meet many friends. One such—Allyn Cecil— invited us to talk at the Sandgate Yacht Club, where we got a formidable reception and, through his son Dave, a regular job working at one of Brisbane's oil refineries. This entailed finding a place to live in town as it was too far to commute from Nobby's house. No problem! Bill Chamberlain, who was to be my foreman, said we could stay in a caravan he had in his garden. Saying goodbye to Nobby and Shrimpy, who was going to stay at Woongoolba Marine, Iris and I moved to Brisbane and into the small but comfortable caravan. In the following months Bill and his wife Betty were to become like mother and father to us. They were perfect examples of the 'real' Australians we came to admire so much. What they lack in European type 'culture' is more than made up for by generosity, bulging hearts and a love of life. Bill's house, in a quiet suburb of Brisbane, was of wood and built on stilts providing space underneath for a games room and pool table. In the garden stood our caravan and an inviting sunken swimming-pool which was the focal point for the neighbourhood kids. There was a well beaten path through to the next door garden of John and Sandra who also became firm friends. For many months, Iris and I luxuriated in this happy atmosphere while, all the time, I was earning lots of lovely dollars at a job in which the climate made work easy and interesting.

In Australia the pubs are a male reserve and I was often forced—not too unwillingly—to spend some time in one on my way home from work. I was not too keen on Australian pubs or 'hotels' as they call them, because they all look too clinical and the type of beer the Aussies drink and the speed they drink it reinforces the hospital impression. It was after one of these 'sessions' that I returned home quite woosy and read in the paper that Prince Philip was to visit Brisbane in the near future. Knowing him to be a yachting man and thinking the publicity would not harm us in our negotiations with the immigration officials, I sat down and wrote him a letter asking if he'd like to visit Shrimpy. Sober, next day, I asked Iris where the letter was that I had jokingly written. She replied that she had jokingly posted it! I was a bit worried because I couldn't remember exactly what I had put in it, but it must have been all right because, a few days later, we received a reply saying he was very interested. As Shrimpy was too far away from Brisbane, I decided that it would be fun to put her on display for the Duke in Bill's swimming-pool. We had been asked to keep quiet about the visit, but we had to tell Bill and Nobby who were tickled pink and helped us move Shrimpy over and into Bill's pool, where she sat quite happily with about a foot to spare at each end. This manoeuvre caused quite a stir in the neighbourhood especially when we put up the mast and sails! But we kept mum about our reasons, despite all the questions. Early on the morning of the 'visit' the neighbours were again startled; waking up to find their street had been closed to hordes of motor-cycle police. All soon became clear when the Royal Rolls pulled up outside Bill's house, followed by a coachload of photographers and TV cameras.

The neighbours poured out of their houses to welcome Prince Philip to their quiet suburb, trampling Bill's back garden completely flat in the process. The Duke made his way to the edge of the swimming pool, where I was introduced to him, and in turn introduced Iris, Nobby, Bill and, of course, Shrimpy! Prince Philip seemed very impressed with Shrimpy and the voyage she had made, but as to the sanity of me, the man who had dared to sail her so far, I think he had grave doubts, understandably so perhaps for his experiences of sailing are worlds apart from mine!

As we got to know the City of Brisbane, we discovered that it was quite a beautiful place—as far as cities go. Well spread out with plenty of greenery between the houses. It took us a fair while to get used to all the noise and bustle after so long in the tiny islands of the Pacific and to cross a main road was a very scary business! We lapped up cinema shows and theatre visits, but were unhappy to notice that all the dreary advertising had scarcely changed since we left civilisation. In the wonderful botanical gardens stretching along the river bank we re-met yachts we had seen out in the Pacific islands and made friends with new ones. Perhaps the most memorable visit was to the zoo. We took one ride up river by steamer and spent the afternoon wandering amongst kangaroos, dingos, emus and various other strange Australian animals, but the show-stealers were the little koala bears, so beautiful, lazy and snuggly-looking—but with very ferocious claws.

An aeroplane ride along the famous Gold Coast, south of Brisbane, gave us a view which impressed us not one little bit, overcrowded and full of all the worst aspects, imported direct from Miami. Inland from Brisbane we discovered the country was still very beautiful and very empty, especially up in the cool green Darling Downs beyond Toowoomba.

*   *   *

By now Iris and I were beginning to get itchy feet again; we were quite rich compared to our usual state and had had more than enough work for a while. Nobby had come up with an amazing offer; he wanted to keep Shrimpy and, in exchange, give me a 30-foot aluminium yacht he was building. This was very tempting and I thought hard about it but in the end I decided to continue sailing with Shrimpy—for many reasons but mainly because I was in love with my boat—and it was a very deep love affair. Iris agreed that I had made the right decision and I think Nobby, although extremely unhappy, understood why I had to turn down his offer.

I gave up my job and we moved back to Woongoolba to prepare Shrimpy for her next voyage. We decided we could afford an outboard and that it would help considerably as we were now leaving the trade winds. Nobby found us a very cheap, but reliable Seagull and eventually, gleaming with new paint, Shrimpy was placed back into the water. A few days before we were ready to leave, a man called Ken Swan visited us and told us that he was the organiser of the Brisbane Yacht Spectacular which was a large annual exhibition of new yachts— rather like the Earl's Court Boat Show—but with the yachts all afloat in Brisbane's large swimming pool. He wanted Shrimpy as the star attraction. I told him I was sorry but we had decided to sail in a few days and were not interested. He was very persistent and keen to have Shrimpy so more to keep him quiet than anything else, I said 'OK we will come—provided you agree to pay the cost of having Shrimpy transported back to Brisbane from wherever we are along the coast when the show starts, pay our expenses plus a substantial appearance fee, plus transport back to that same spot on the coast after the show.'

'There', I thought, 'that's telling him'. But, to my surprise, without any hesitation or argument he said, 'Agreed'.

As a shake-down cruise I sailed Shrimpy, with the help of Nobby's son, Leslie, the 30-odd miles to Sandgate Yacht Club. From there Shrimpy would take her official leave of Brisbane. The yacht club did us proud and all our wonderful Aussie friends piled into numerous motorboats and escorted us out of the harbour and on our way. Au revoir beautiful Brisbane.

13

Behind the Barrier Reef
April 20–September 17 1977

Leaving the bustle of Brisbane behind us, we set off—but not very far. About 15 miles further north we found a nice little anchorage in a bay at the mouth of a river, cooked lunch and then settled down to re-tune ourselves to the slow-paced luxurious life on a yacht in warm tropical seas.

For once we had good, large-scale charts and I took them out to study our intended route. It looked very promising—we had decided to sail very slowly along the coast from Brisbane right up to Cape York, the northern-most tip of Australia. We had the Barrier Reef to protect us and ensure calm seas all the way, the wind should be behind us most of the time, there were hundreds of little islands and many interesting-looking rivers. Above all, there was space to breathe—only two towns of any significance on the whole 1,500 miles of coastline! For safe yet beautiful holiday sailing, forget the bumpy Caribbean, the crowded, expensive Med, the remoteness of the Pacific, go sail 'behind the Barrier Reef'. The charts I was dreamily poring over contained a strange mixture of English and Aboriginal names—Ipswich for example is just east of Toowoomba, while Mooloolaba is just south of Mary-borough. Captain Cook also had his share of fun, such as Weary Bay, across which his crew had to row the *Endeavour,* and Cape Tribulation which was in sight when *Endeavour* was wrecked and almost lost on a coral reef.

Next day, we had a nice sail to reach the snug little marina of Mooloolaba, very crowded with yachts and not too interesting but convenient for storing up. We went to the local supermarket and purchased a huge amount of food—it's amazing just how much we can store away in Shrimpy. The store manager allowed us to use two of his wheeled shopping baskets to get it all down to the boat—it's quite a problem pushing those trolleys along an unpaved road without breaking any eggs!

Our next stop was Noosaville on the Noosa river—a small, shallow, swampy backwater. There was quite a swell and the complicated entrance to the river, across a constantly shifting bar, looked very risky, but after sailing up and down having a good look, I decided to try it. We made it safely, not without a few hairy moments, and found good anchorage in the pretty little river. The next morning we found we had trapped ourselves, for the weather had deteriorated and the bar would be impossible for a few days. We were quite content to wait for a while; there was no hurry, the more so after we met Merv and Dorothy, owners of a small hotel who, with great generosity, offered us moorings for Shrimpy alongside the hotel and installed us in one of their luxurious rooms all for free and, come the weekend, when the place was packed they forbade us to move back on to Shrimpy which we had intended to do so that they could hire 'our' room.

We went exploring the shallow lakes in Merv's powerboat and two of his guests took us on a tour of the hinterland. When the bar had calmed down enough, we sailed out leaving many friends behind. Merv had even arranged for the local safety boat to make sure we crossed the bar without problems.

Further along the coast we anchored at Rainbow Sands, an area of huge sand dunes backed by rain forest. This is the area where the four-wheel drive owners come to play, whizzing along the multi-coloured sandy beach or through the forest on tracks no ordinary car could manage. These Landrovers, Toyotas, etc, had bounced over hundreds of miles of rough track to get here, most with a speedboat trailing behind and a big tent lashed to the roof. Their main traffic hazard was kangaroos, wallabies and the occasional aeroplane or helicopter which had landed for a weekend picnic.

Iris and I climbed up to the lighthouse at the top of the headland to have a chat with the lighthouse keeper and, by the time we got back to the beach, there was quite a large surf rolling in. Shrimpy was safe enough, protected by the headland, but it was going to be quite a job to get through the surf with the dinghy so we eventually decided that Iris would spend the night ashore in a tent with some of the people we had met there, while I struggled out to Shrimpy half in and half out of the dinghy.

We had to wait a few days before we could move on, for our next anchorage lay between a huge 60-mile long sand dune called Fraser Island, and the coast. Once there, we were within the protection of the Barrier Reef but the entrance had a shallow bar—impassable with these seas. Eventually Iris rejoined Shrimpy and we crossed the bar without problem. In the calm waters behind Fraser Island we ran aground just after high tide and were well and truly stuck. As the waters receded, we found we were sitting on the highest little sandbank in the whole area! We used the time before the tide returned to clean Shrimpy's bottom—omitting to tell astonished locals that it was not fantastic powers of navigation, but pure chance that landed us in this perfect ship-cleaning position.

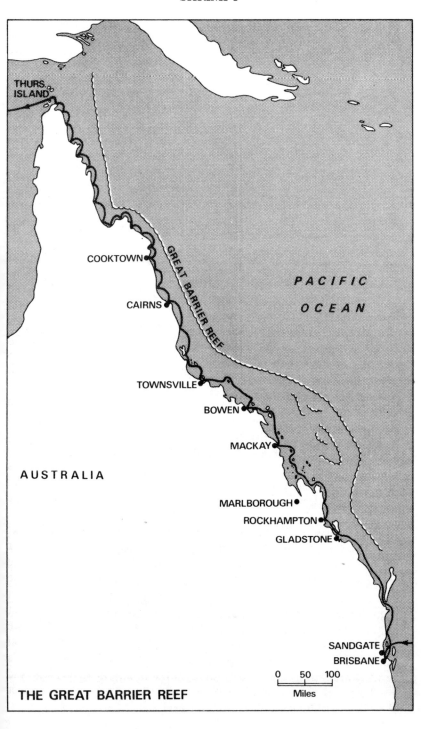

THE GREAT BARRIER REEF

SHRIMPY

Sailing northwards, stopping each night in a snug anchorage, we eventually reached the pretty little town of Gladstone. It was now time for the Brisbane Yacht Spectacular, so I 'phoned Ken Swan and told him where we were. Everything was soon arranged, Shrimpy, loaded on to a truck set off to Brisbane by road, while Iris and I boarded a train to go by rail. On arrival in Brisbane, we renewed all our acquaintances except for Bill and Betty who—perhaps catching our itchy feet disease—had gone to Canada for a year. But John and Sandra, their neighbours, now became our hosts; this was much better than a hotel.

The yacht show was a success despite some cold weather. Shrimpy now sitting in her second swimming pool, put up bravely with two more weeks of being thumped by 'experts' and Iris perfected her fake smile. I amused myself by listening to the salesman next to us trying to convince prospective buyers that his plastic tub, the same size as Shrimpy, was also her equal in strength and design—I wouldn't have sailed across a pond in it! By the show's end, we were very ready to get back to the quiet of little Gladstone harbour.

Shrimpy back in the sea again, we continued north from Gladstone alternating our nightly anchorages between coast and islands. Because of the beauty and climate of this sparsely populated Queensland coast it naturally attracts many characters, from hippy communes to hermits, interspersed with quiet, retired couples who want a simple easy-going life. One of these characters was an old man who fell in love with pretty little Gould Island and decided to live there. The only trouble was that this was national park land, so the poor chap was chucked off his island each time the officials visited it. After a few years and many evictions later, the officials decided that the only thing to do was make the old man a park ranger—so now he has his island and an income to go with it.

On Beautiful Percy Island lives Englishman, Andrew Martin. All the yachts visit this island—as did Shrimpy. It has a beautiful natural harbour and Andrew welcomes yachties; he has even run a freshwater pipeline down to the beach and erected a 'picnic hut' for them. But try as he may, he cannot find anyone to share his island; everyone who has tried it has found it too lonely It was on this beach that we met the lighthouse keeper from the next island—a mere 500 yards away. He was on his annual holiday, so he had moved his family and most of his furniture from his luxury house by the lighthouse across into an old tent on this beach. It took him about ten trips with his little dinghy and will take another ten trips to get all the stuff back in a couple of weeks' time! Bedarra Island was settled by two Americans, one called Hip and the other Hooray. Arthur has the most beautiful view in Queensland (his own words) from his isolated house at the mouth of Bailey Creek—and a bottle of 'home brew' each evening. The hippy commune at Cedar Bay—although miles from everywhere—had recently been attacked by a sea-borne assault and had their houses burnt to the ground by a detachment of the Cairns police force.

All along the coast, nature mingles danger with beauty—turtles and dugongs mix with crocodiles, sea snakes and sharks, pretty luminous corals and anemones hide stone fish and poisonous shells. Ashore, the terrible Gympie tree grows alongside beautiful orchids. Cassowaries and kangaroos roam the bush, competing with the less exotic but equally wild goats and pigs. At dawn and dusk, the mosquito reigns supreme.

The only touristy spots anything like crowded along this coast are the Whitsunday Islands and Cairns. The former for the pseudo-isolation of hideaway hotels and the latter for game fishing. At Cairns we took the fantastic but touristy tram ride up into the mountains of the Atherton table-land, in order to see the sea from a different angle for a change.

A bit further north from Cairns is Cooktown. This little village is the end of the road for normal vehicles; the whole of the Cape York peninsula has nothing more than a few rough tracks. Loaded down with stores from Cooktown, we sailed through the maze of reef and islands which become denser towards Cape York, the tip of Australia. Each night we anchored behind a reef or in a bay, exploring ashore wherever it looked interesting, catching fish to barbecue on completely deserted sandy beaches that stretch for miles with rarely a footprint.

There are only two hamlets on the 300-mile stretch of coastline between Cooktown and Cape York. The southernmost, called Portland Roads, provided us with quite a surprise, for here the population was a mere 16 people, yet one couple knew Iris's brother's wife's sister (work that out!). It sounds complicated but is an amazing coincidence nonetheless. Needless to say, as soon as this was discovered, we were doubly welcomed at the settlement. The only connection with the outside world was via a very rough track passable only by a four-wheel drive vehicle and only in the dry season. The people there are mainly retired couples looking for a simple life; they have certainly found it! The only other settlement was at the mouth of the Escape river, where a small colony of Japanese were engaged in farming cultured pearls. As we zig-zagged Shrimpy through the rows of anchored pearl rafts to their jetty, we could see a large sign. It said 'Keep Out', 'Private Property', 'No Visitors'. We tied up to the jetty anyway. The sign turned out to be a bluff, for we were treated with all the restrained kindness the orient is noted for.

With the wind behind us, pushing Shrimpy merrily along, we eventually arrived at Cape York. This was a great turning point for Shrimpy as from here we could sail westwards once more! One would expect the tip of such a great land to be rugged and rocky, not so Cape York. A delightful sandy bay provided so smooth an anchorage that we could beach Shrimpy without problem. We camped ashore at this pretty spot for three days for, unlike the top of Snowdon and other inaccessible British places, there was no cafe to spoil the view! There was a rough track, however, which winds through the enormous three-metre high ant hills which abound there and along this track at reasonably regular intervals would arrive a four-wheel drive van, loaded to the roof with people and possessions. Each of these arrivals without fail had the sides of their vans plastered with the words 'Cape York or Bust' and the strange thing was that when they arrived they would stay less than an hour and then set off home to whichever far flung Australian city they had come from. Some did not even get out of their vans!

From Cape York we set off on the 30-mile trip to the group of islands that guard the eastern entrance to the notorious Torres Strait. Thursday Island, the main but smallest island of this group, nestles (not unnaturally) between Wednesday Island and Friday Island. On the chart the main harbour seemed to be safe and snug and protected from all sides. This was not so, for here is the shallow meeting place between two oceans—the Pacific and the Indian—and where two oceans meet you get currents. In the narrow channels around these islands the current often runs up to ten knots. As Shrimpy's top speed was only five, you can imagine the fun we had. We had been looking forward to our visit to Thursday Island because many Australians we had talked to regarded it as their own tame Pacific island paradise. How disappointed we were! The place was hot, dry and barren, no fruit, no flowers. The town uncared for, broken bottles and rubbish was strewn all over the place—the whole scene gave an aura of decay. There was just no comparison to beautiful Fiji, Tonga and Polynesia and the Thursday Islanders, living off government handouts, cannot hold a candle to those who live off the handouts of nature. Surprisingly enough, all the inhabitants seemed very happy and friendly despite their environment. As the main harbour was extremely uncomfortable, because of the strong currents, we sailed Shrimpy across to nearby Prince of Wales Island and found a much calmer anchorage. We had assumed we could go shopping on Thursday Island by ferry as the main airport was on Prince of Wales Island, but we had forgotten one more curse of these islands—their prices! The ferry fare for the one mile trip cost £4, not really surprising as petrol here cost £1 a quart.

Luckily, there was one small shop on Prince of Wales Island where we could obtain supplies and its owner was very interested in yachties. A curious sign on the shop door of this rather individual storekeeper said: 'All dogs entering this shop will be shot'. I was relieved to find out that it didn't apply to seadogs!

On leaving this island, which we did rapidly because of the ugliness of the group, we were faced with our longest sail since leaving Brisbane. This consisted of the 350-mile passage across the top of the Gulf of Carpenteria. The shallow areas which extend many miles westwards of Thursday Island and hamper moderately draughted ships considerably, didn't bother us at all for the sea was calm and clear. Shrimpy, with a mere two-foot draught, has no echo sounder and I work on the principle of what I can't see, I won't hit. This only becomes scary in the dirty waters of populated coastlines, or at night.

For the first day, we had the wind we expected—light and from behind us. It was perfect; blue sky, gentle sea and reasonable speed. Early in the morning on the second day of the voyage, we turned on the radio for the weather forecast: 'Strong gale expected', it said, 'Southwest winds 40–45 knots, seas very rough.' Iris and I looked at each other, then turned away quickly, for news like that is unbearable on the nerves. Furthermore, we had every right to expect gentle south-easterly winds for the gulf is notedly a placid sea at this time of year.

By mid-afternoon the blow had started and we began to get seasick. It lasted for three days, the waves in that shallow gulf became steeper than any I had ever seen. They were not particularly high like the giant Pacific rollers but much more dangerous, as it was like being hit repeatedly by a brick wall. For three days we hung on battered, damp and lost because, although the sun was often out, I couldn't keep still enough to get a sight with the sextant. After the gale passed, the waves died down amazingly fast and soon we were wondering if it had all been a bad dream—provided we didn't look at the jumbled mess on the cabin floor. Then, after two days of perfect weather and good sights, land emerged from the sea exactly when and where I had reckoned it should and we could just pick out the harbour entrance of Gove before darkness fell.

On the headland of Gove there is a huge bauxite plant and its myriad lights, looking like a fairground, would make it easy to enter the harbour at night, or so I thought . . .

As the wind died down and we slowly ghosted our way towards the harbour, we suddenly saw a great flash of light and heard a huge explosion. Five minutes after this every single light ashore went out and safety valves by the thousand blew steam at the sky. As if blinded, we found ourselves in total darkness surrounded by man-made fog and the smell of burnt out electrics. My first reaction to this eerie experience (rather silly with hindsight) was to look over the side of the boat to see if we had cut a cable! Before we had time to get really worried, the lights ashore came on again and we anchored in the harbour with no further problem. It had been a very hard sail and we slept all through the next day—which, incidentally, happened to be my thirty-first birthday.

14

Gove
September 17 1977–June 10 1978

It had taken us six months to sail along the beautiful Queensland coast from Brisbane to Gove and the next hurricane season was fast approaching so it was time to start looking for winter moorings and work. We had not sailed very far this last season but we were in no hurry to go anywhere: if you're as free as a bird, there is no need to flap your wings too hard. It was, therefore, with enquiring eyes that we emerged from Shrimpy's cabin—after a well-earned rest—to look about the beautiful, perfectly protected anchorage of Gove Harbour. We knew nothing about the place, for all Australians we had asked knew only that bauxite was mined there. The enormous plant and loading complex was very evident and as much an eyesore as such places must, by nature, be, but the sheer amount of virgin bushland surrounding the bay seemed to dwarf this achievement of man. In fact, apart from the plant, bush was all we could see. Suddenly, in a remote corner of the bay, a sail bloomed, then another and eventually we made out a group of little dinghies so we upped anchor and sailed over to see what was there.

Gove Yacht Club turned out to be one of the smallest but also one of the best we have ever visited. We were welcomed by the commodore of the club who immediately gave us a key to the showers and lounge room, plus use of a refrigerator and the run of the premises—which included a nice little workshop and, although dinghy racing was underway, he even found time to drive us into town for a guided tour! The town exists solely because of the mine. It is a unique place in many ways: it has been carved out of virgin bush and the only way in is by plane or private boat (unless you fancy a really rough trek through the bush). The town has all the usual government departments, plus a pub, shop, hotel, school and huge sports complex surrounded by houses, flats and a single-men's hostel. All laid out with much thought, well away from the plant in air-conditioned, mosquito-proofed luxury. The main roads in town and to and from the airport and plant are all surfaced, but if you want to set foot off the beaten track, it is four-wheel drive territory—even to the nearby aborigine mission station. There is no shortage of water, happily, so in the hot, dry season the town uses

Right *Watch out for the big ones! We approach Brisbane harbour.*

Below *Our arrival at Brisbane does not go unheralded.*

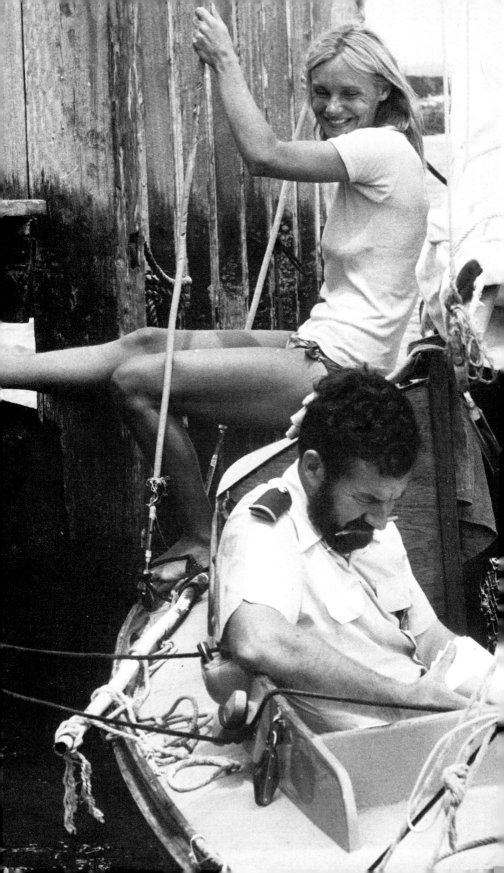

Left *Boarded by Customs officers—but only one at a time!* **Above** *At Brisbane we meet 'Nobby' C.E. Clark, the man who built Shrimpy back in England, many years ago.* **Below** *Crowded Brisbane, no place for a yacht like Shrimpy.*

Left *At Norman Park, Brisbane, Shrimpy is placed in a backyard swimming pool . . .*

Below left *. . . proudly wearing her unique running sail plus plain sail . . .*

Right *. . . for an informal visit by Prince Philip, who looks rather bemused . . .*

Below *. . . as he inspects the yacht and hears of her amazing voyage.*

Above *Looking like a fish out of water, Shrimpy is put on display at various shopping complexes in Australia.* **Below** *Ready to leave Brisbane to put out to sea again, and not looking too unhappy about the prospect!*

Above *As we set sail from Brisbane the Sandgate Club motorboats provide an escort for us.*
Below *Shrimpy lifts her bow to demonstrate her planing abilities!* **Overleaf** *Rather cramped for space as we entertain friends on board at Noosa, Australia.*

more water per head of population than anywhere else in Australia—in the wet season they almost drown! Everything in Gove is naturally very expensive, even the Woolworths supermarket, but high wages and fringe benefits such as free air fares and virtually free accommodation, make life for those who work for the main company very easy indeed. Not quite so fortunate are the rare visitors and handful of sub-contractors who live in a village of prefabs and unpaved roads just out of town and who are a bit cramped for space—except when compared to Shrimpy.

In all, it seemed a perfect place to make a quick fortune and then leave before falling prey to the petty backbiting and nastiness which is human nature in this, as in any other crowded, isolated community. Now, if only Iris or I can find employment . . . A week later, we were both hard at work for one of the local sub-contractors—John Graham—dismantling old prefabs for construction elsewhere. The pay was good and the work fun—like playing with a huge Meccano set and John, our boss, with his 'cavalier' attitude to life, was easy to work for. This job finished, John put me to work digging holes in the airport, while Iris started to work on Shrimpy who was due for a good refit.

Meanwhile, four other yachts had arrived to sit out the hurricane season in Gove. The crews of all the yachts found as much work as they wanted, sooner or later. We became great friends with Bill and his young Indonesian wife, Etty, on one of the yachts. Bill, though a very likeable fellow, was very much the 'male chauvinist' Aussie, but his wife, aided and abetted by Iris, was slowly and subtly changing him. Another yacht—a beautiful old converted Indonesian workboat—contained 'Peter the Pom', his wife Avis and a whole load of kids. Peter—a larger than life character—was an engraver and locksmith and quite an adventurer. He had taken his family around Australia in a double-decker bus working as he went, but now they were travelling by sea and, as they were quite new to it, I spent some time helping him with his navigation. I tried to dispel some of the ridiculous advice he had been given—by some of those many 'experts' who never get their feet wet—on the inadvisability of sailing without club burgee at the top of the mast, or a 'go fast' stripe along the side of the boat, etc.

The yacht club was quite a way from town so, as we were quickly growing rich, we bought an old jalopy to move around in. We had many friends to visit; all the wonderfully helpful generous yacht club members and especially for Iris, the Swiss members of the community of which there were many, as the mining company was Swiss owned! Car, work . . . all we needed to complete the picture was a house! We put a note on the town notice board saying we would look after house, pets, garden, etc, for anyone who was going on holiday. Presto! For the rest of our time in Gove we didn't spend one more day living on

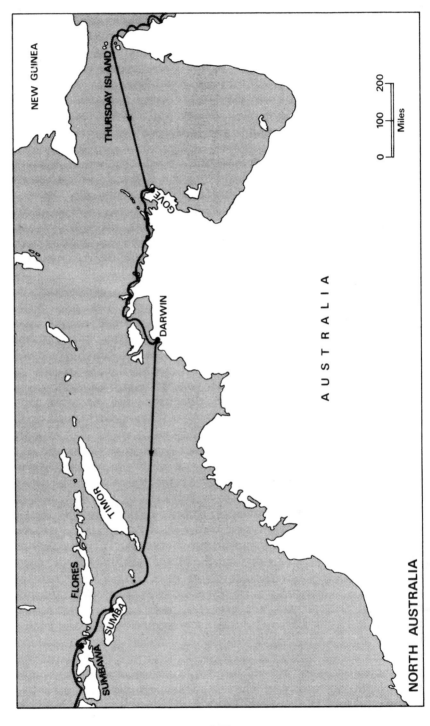

Shrimpy but every fortnight would simply move from one luxurious house to the next!

The yacht club's sailing season was drawing to a close, not so much because of the weather but more the deadly jellyfish called 'stingers' which approach the coast at this time of year. They are almost invisible and if they brush against the main trunk of the body, it is usually fatal, even a small sting on the hand or foot can cause many weeks of agony and we were advised to wear pantyhose when wading through the water to and from Shrimpy.

Shrimpy joined in the end of season regatta and won her race—not, I hasten to add, through racing skill but solely due to an overgenerous handicapper! Then, with the aid and permission of the yacht club, we took her out of the water and put her in their compound to make her doubly safe for the hurricane season. We also took the opportunity to replace Shrimpy's 15-year old keel-bolts which were oozing rust, with brand new stainless steel ones made especially by Deiter and Hans, two of our yacht club friends.

Just before Christmas, John ran out of work for me to do but I was only unemployed for a week before I had a job in the single-men's hostel kitchen, provided by one of our Swiss acquaintances—John Keagi—who was the catering sub-contractor and who, with his wife Emily, became firm friends. With this job went a room in the hostel and we used it to store all Shrimpy's gear while we painted her.

Days passed quickly and happily in this—for us—strange lifestyle. We were constantly surprised at things like hot running water and lights that went on and off at the flick of a switch. Of course you never actually forget about these sort of things but after a long period without them, their rediscovery really fascinates you!

We started exploring the countryside with a borrowed four-wheel drive but were scared to go too far into the bush in case the truck became bogged. The land is covered in the main by gum trees and thick bush; the aborigines often set fire to the land to clear the undergrowth and flush out game; often the night sky is ablaze with deliberately set bush fires. Surprisingly, this does not harm the gum trees, in fact with many species, their seeds will not germinate until they have been passed through fire.

The aborigines, themselves, wander aimlessly between the mission and the town because the majority, very sadly, have been trapped by a mixture of the white man's religion and alcohol and are an apathetic bunch.

One of the houses we looked after belonged to the port pilot and one day he took me out with him to show me what manoeuvring a big ship was like. As we stood together on the bridge of a huge ore carrier and he casually murmured orders to the helmsman to bring us gently

123

alongside the terminal, it was hard to compare to the fast jerky movements of barely organised panic that accompanies Shrimpy's entrances into port!

As the hurricane season drew to a close, the itchy feet syndrome began again; we started going to night school, where an enterprising teacher was giving Indonesian lessons—because Indonesia would be our next country.

Work in the kitchen was getting harder and harder for me as I daydreamed of future horizons. Eventually I could stand it no longer. I handed in my resignation, we sold our car, put Shrimpy—shining clean—back in the water, moved all our paraphernalia back on board, plus food, plus a nice new dinghy and lots of other goodies and with many wishes of good luck and bon voyage, we were on our way once more.

*   *   *

We left Gove on May 1 1978, with enough money to get us right to the Mediterranean without having to look for work on the way. Our next main port was to be Darwin which was about 300 miles along the coast of Arnhemland. This huge area of land is aborigine reserve and whites are only allowed in by special permission. There are no roads, no towns and only a couple of mission stations. The coastline is very shallow, the water very murky and there are also big tides, strong currents and whirlpools—for these reasons most yachts give the area a wide berth, but we decided that it would be safe enough for tiny Shrimpy with her shallow draught to stick close to the shore and explore this little-known coast—it would also be much more fun.

On leaving Gove, our first problem was to pass through the Wessel Islands. These stick many miles out from the coastline and have two or three navigable passes between them, but the tidal rips and races have put paid to many boats much bigger and sturdier than little Shrimpy. We did not even consider the most notorious of these passes called the 'hole in the wall' which is deep and full of whirlpools; instead we decided to try a much shallower but wider one nearer the coast. Picking our tides carefully, we just made it through, more by luck than judgment, as the muddy waters made it impossible to pick out the deepest channel. In calm water behind the islands we closed the coast looking for a break in the mangrove trees—for if my chart was accurate we could sail the next 30 miles or so through connecting lagoons and rivers in the mangrove swamp.

Finding the entrance proved quite easy, but we had to wait for high tide to get in and even with only two-foot draught, Shrimpy bumped a few times going over the bar at the mouth of the river. Once inside the

124

swamp, the river deepened and narrowed until the mangroves almost met, forming an archway of impenetrable greenery.

Sailing among mangroves is always very eerie—it is impossible to get ashore for at high tide there *is* no shore, just tangled unbreakable root systems, and at low tide mud too liquified to support a human. A compass is virtually useless as the channel meanders so much with hundreds of offshoots leading nowhere. The dark dank vegetation is alive with all manner of strange noises that echo startlingly in the stillness. Nevertheless, it is beautiful in its own way—providing you have enough mosquito repellent to enjoy it!

Hating to disturb the quietness with the outboard, Iris and I spent two days just drifting with the current through this maze of channels, occasionally shoving a paddle into the water to keep us in mid-stream. Drifting forwards, backwards or sideways we sat in the cockpit watching the wildlife which consisted mainly of mating couples of the beautiful sea eagles, busily engaged in making their enormous nests, while across the water surface wriggled numerous poisonous sea snakes and an occasional saltwater crocodile.

Eventually we reached the sea once more and set sail along the coast. We managed to find a calm protected anchorage each night; beautiful sandy beaches where the only human footprints were our own. We warily shared waterholes with the wild 'cape buffalo', cattle, horses and all manner of small crawly things. For weeks the world seemed to be ours alone, but all too soon Darwin loomed over the horizon and our first contact with civilisation was a military patrol boat which, thinking we were a refugee boat from Vietnam, came charging over to have a closer look and, with not so much as a wave, sped right past us leaving Shrimpy bouncing uncomfortably in his enormous wake.

The anchorage at Darwin Yacht Club left much to be desired, not well protected and because of the huge tides, yachts have to anchor a long way offshore, but the friendliness of the club outweighed its miserable anchorage and we were soon made to feel quite at home. The club is, thankfully, a fair distance from the city of Darwin which is a characterless, hot, noisy place which has no real reason for its existence and is mainly occupied, therefore, by non-productive people—the majority being government officials. Paradoxically, perhaps, the people are much happier, polite and helpful than is the case in most cities—even the officials we had to do business with!

Our long stay in beautiful Australia was fast drawing to a close and we had arranged visas for Indonesia—not the easiest or cheapest thing in the world to do; packed Shrimpy full of stores and water; got clearance from the Port Captain and as the tide began to ebb, we were off.

15

Indonesia—land of islands
June 10–August 11 1978

As we sailed out from Darwin, leaving Australia and all its amazing wealth behind, we thought we had an easy eight day trip ahead of us to reach the island of Sumba, Indonesia. It turned out to be, however, one of the most eventful passages we have made. Things started happening no more than ten miles out to sea, still just in sight of land, when Iris—who was steering at the time—dug me out of the cabin and a good book with one of her 'something's wrong' screams. As I scrambled on deck, wondering whether it was shoals, sharks or oil tankers—the three most common 'scares'—I saw something completely different. It was a little motorboat with a broken outboard, at anchor; its four occupants desperately waving a fishing rod with a red shirt tied to the end of it! Approaching them, we began to wonder and worry about the method of rescue. It would be impossible for little Shrimpy to tow them back to Australia against the wind and current and impossible to take them all aboard Shrimpy. So we had two alternatives: either to stay with them and attract the attention of a larger boat with our flares, or to tow them to Indonesia! They didn't think much of the second alternative at all. Luckily, an easy solution arrived just after we did. An Air Force reconnaissance plane, which was patrolling the area looking for Vietnamese refugee boats, had also seen the make-shift distress flag and, after buzzing around for a while sizing up the situation, they dropped a message container. With an uncannily accurate shot it landed only a few feet from our two tiny boats but the current was so swift that we had to sail Shrimpy off to catch it. The message read, 'If you still need assistance wave the red flag again'. We shouted over to our distressees that they should do this. Within a short time, we saw a Navy patrol boat charging towards us, so we left the little motorboat to their professional rescuers, telling them the big sea was no place for small powerboats. It's a good job I couldn't hear their reply!

Later that same evening, the wind died completely so, leaving the sails up and flapping aimlessly, Iris and I went to bed. About midnight, we were rudely awakened by a blinding light shining into the cabin. Frightened and still half asleep, I staggered on deck. As my senses cleared I discovered that the light was a searchlight attached to a Navy boat—probably the same one which had rescued our friends earlier on—and it was right alongside us. The silence was very loud, so I just sat naked in the cockpit and stared at the searchlight. Eventually, an amplified voice came out of the darkness—'Turn your lights on'. Resisting the temptation to strike a match, I held up our 'Woolies' special torch and flashed it a couple of times. Again the silence was loud, then—'Is that all you have?'. I nodded. Another long silence, then, without another word, the searchlight snapped off and the patrol boat slowly moved away—the poor Captain must have been at a loss for words!

The next morning it was the weather's turn to harrass us and, as Darwin radio began to issue gale warnings, the wind complied, building up steep seas which came rolling down on us from all sides and we were playing submarines for the next three days. Badly seasick in this sudden rough patch of weather, I was very lackadaisical with my navigation. As a result, we found that when the storm had abated we were about 200 miles off course and had a long, hard headwind sail to reach Sumba. For all this distance, we were constantly drenched by monsoonal rains and felt really down in the dumps. But soon the miracle happened (as they do so frequently at sea) and the sun came out, the gentle trade winds returned, the beautiful island of Sumba rose over the horizon and quite suddenly we found ourselves sailing along the coast to Waingapu harbour in company with many elegant 'prahus', local vessels which sail the waters of Indonesia without an engine amongst them.

Then came the operation that sailing is all about: dropping anchor in a snug harbour in a brand new country, observing, smelling and tasting a new, strange way of life. As we sat in the centre of the harbour waiting for practique, the Indonesian courtesy flag flapping on the mast was the twenty-first different country flag we had flown, the twenty-first different country we had visited—Shrimpy had come of age!

It took about a day to finish all the paperwork required by the customs, immigration officials, harbour-master, etc, etc,—and we were later to discover that this was usual for every Indonesian port we visited. Indeed anything official took hours to do; not because they were busy or sadistic, but because they were usually off somewhere playing cards or sitting in the sun without a care in the world and when eventually tracked down, were much more interested in chatting than filling out forms. But we were in no hurry either!

After obtaining clearance, we found a snug anchorage amid a myriad of prahus. These classical Indonesian sailing vesels have to be seen to be believed. With no motors to aid them, they take turns to manoeuvre alongside a tiny jetty, load so much cargo that they are awash and then allow passengers on board, to perch precariously on top of everything. The mooring lines are then cast off, the enormous sails raised and away they go—but so slowly it often takes three or four hours just to get out of the harbour. In this fashion, the bulk of Indonesia's inter-island trade is carried, with only a few large cargo ships to help out.

We pumped up our little plastic dinghy and rowed ashore, to be met by a crowd of kids who were fascinated by this strange type of craft and who could not understand our protests when they took to bouncing up and down on the inflatable as it rested on the sharp stones of the beach. We eventually had to cart it to the local police station for safe keeping.

Walking around Waingapu, the main town of Sumba Island, we found life moving along at a slow, easy pace. Horse-drawn carts still compete—comfortably so—with clapped out minibuses, for carrying both goods and passengers. As we strolled in the market place making use of basic Indonesian and sign language, we attracted large crowds of children, each one of whom knows two words of English—'Hello Mister!'—which they would scream at the top of their voices to Iris or me, accompanied with an enormous grin. Our reply of 'salamat pagi' turned the grins into gales of laughter. No one gestured or asked for money, everyone was poor but happy.

Then into a restaurant for our first taste of Indonesian food: large plates of rice aided and abetted by small but delicious side dishes of meat, eggs and fish plus an assortment of spices almost too hot to handle and washed down with glasses of tea 'manis'.

Later that evening, lazing in Shrimpy's cockpit, basking in the warm sunset, an item of yachting news on the radio caused me to wonder about those yachtsmen who sail non-stop around the world in under a year—chasing some strange hypothetical record of masochistic endurance and whether they have any inkling of all they are missing. They would be as happy jogging round a running track until they dropped!

*　　　*　　　*

Leaving Sumba, we set sail towards Sumbawa Island. As night fell, we found ourselves entering the strait between Sumbawa and Komodo Island of the famed dragons. We sailed all night but by morning had barely moved an inch, so strong were the currents against us! As day broke, the wind began to die and we lost hundreds of yards of expensive rope, trying to anchor in deep water to avoid being pushed backwards. Then behind us and rapidly approaching on a very erratic course, we saw a local sailing vessel and we followed him through the strait—he must have known the currents like the back of his hand as he meandered from back-eddy to back-eddy.

Soon we had left the strait with all its turbulence behind and were sailing amid many local craft towards the sunset and the beautiful little village of Bima. The chain of mountainous Indonesian islands became greener and wetter the further west we sailed and the next island we visited, Lombok, was perhaps the most beautiful that we visited. In the safe landlocked harbour we met *Sunshine*, a ten-metre yacht with Max and Brenda on board and, after chatting for a while, we decided to join forces to spend four days hiking in the sparsely populated mountainous part of the island. Max had all the gear needed for such an expedition and was able to lend Iris and me a two-man tent, rucksack, etc; we also felt very safe with him, for he had previously climbed the north face of the Eiger!

In order to avoid a long walk through the flat rice fields before we reached the distant volcanoes, we decided to go by Bemo and had our first taste of Indonesia's answer to the public transport problem. The Bemo is a small van, its rear fitted with seats, windows and an open doorway at the back, plus a huge luggage rack on top. It is capable of carrying about ten people, all their shopping or market produce, plus pigs, chickens, etc. In lieu of buses, hundreds of these little Bemos ply the streets of each island; they have definite routes but are willing to make small detours for a few extra pennies. They have no timetable but go as soon as they are full or the driver is bored of standing still, but there are so many that you very rarely have to wait more than a few minutes. If you are rich and impatient you hire one all to yourself at the same price as a taxi. In this fashion—despite Indonesia's terrible roads—their public transport system moves people much faster, more cheaply and provides more jobs than anywhere in England, albeit a scary, non-too-comfortable method of travelling.

By the time we arrived at the foot of the mountains, where the road petered out and the Bemo stopped, it was pouring with rain. Not wanting to get out tents wet so soon, we approached a small wooden house and, before even asking, were invited in for the night, given a meal and put to bed in the main room; the family sleeping in the kitchen. In payment we cooked the breakfast for them and though they weren't too keen on our porridge, etc, they were very intrigued with Max's little petrol stove which eliminated the annoying task of lighting a charcoal fire in very damp conditions.

The rain had stopped in the night and we had a beautiful day as we climbed upwards through the clouds on ridiculously steep rough tracks. We passed many local men on their way down carrying enormous loads of firewood which they had cut out of the forest to sell in the lowlands. How they managed such loads was hard for me to imagine. I tried the weight of one and could hardly lift, let alone walk, with it—they ran!

On reaching the topmost ridge, a beautiful sight met our eyes—a lush green valley lay snuggled between towering peaks of volcanoes—not all extinct—and looking exactly like the 'lost kingdoms' of fiction.

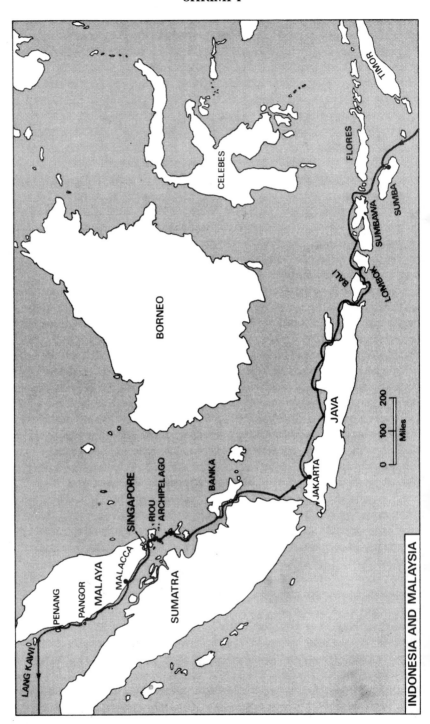

INDONESIA AND MALAYSIA

Two or three thousand people lived in the villages dotted about this amazing valley and they all clustered around us, chatting and laughing at the rare sight of strangers strolling through their land and, when Max got his camera out, he was almost mobbed by young kids wanting to get into the picture.

After two or three days of wonderful walking, more often lost than not, on the many criss-crossing little tracks, we eventually arrived back at the harbour, very tired. Here, an unpleasant surprise awaited for we discovered that, in our absence, Shrimpy had been broken into and the radio and tape recorder were missing. This fact I reported to the police the following morning, just as a formality—I thought—for I had heard many stories of the notorious Indonesian thieves. I was very surprised, therefore, at the amount of official concern and action that my report brought about and astonished when only one day later, the missing items had been found and returned by the chief of police of the port, with a huge happy grin on his face!

A few days later, when our feet and legs were fully recovered from their long and unaccustomed exercise, we sailed the few miles across the strait to the most famous of the Indonesian islands—Bali.

The island, much as we expected, was full of tourists and hotels, but it was pleasantly surprising to find that the tourist industry does not seem to have hurt this island too much. The tourists, seemingly by choice, huddle together in the one small corner of the island which has been 'Europeanised' and provide great entertainment for the locals who derive immense fun from watching acres of sickly-white, naked blubber as it sweats, stinks and sizzles under the hot noon-day sun.

There were many yachts in port, some of which we had met before in various harbours throughout the Pacific and we all went off together one night to watch the legendary 'Balinese dance'. In the cool of an enchanted tropical night, an open air stage provided a magical backdrop as the dancers performed the stories of their gods with such immaculate beauty, it was breathtaking.

Back in the harbour, one of the many enterprising young lads who wander around the yachts in their dinghies, selling carvings, paintings, services and their labour, expressed great surprise at Shrimpy's smallness and asked me to write her name on a piece of paper. I did so and two days later, he returned with a gift for 'the brave little boat'— the words *Super Shrimp* decoratively carved in wood. What a wonderfully thoughtful present. Shrimpy bears it proudly on her stern to this day.

From Bali, I was to be single-handed once more because Iris had decided it was time for her to visit her mother back in Switzerland. It was a sad time for both of us as we had been together now ever since we met way back in Panama, half a world away and togetherness on an

18-foot boat is very close indeed. In all that time we had had never a fight—only a few cross words when we ran out of cigarettes.

We found that the cheapest flight from Indonesia to Switzerland was with Aeroflot and the ticket got Iris safely home—but if you ever ask her what the Aeroflot line is like you better be wearing a suit of armour at the time!

With Iris gone, I felt very lonely and empty. Bali didn't seem at all romantic or mysterious anymore. I quickly began preparing Shrimpy for departure and early next morning, I was off. Iris had arranged to return to Shrimpy when I reached the Mediterranean—it looked an awful long way away.

16

Single-handed again
August 11 1978–January 3 1979

Leaving the main port of Bali, I sailed along the southern side of the island and into the narrow Bali strait—between Bali and Java. It was hard work learning to sail alone again—even with the assistance of the brand new five horse-power Yamaha outboard which we had bought in Lombok, for now I was leaving the trade winds behind and it would take forever to reach the Med without a motor, especially in the Red Sea. No longer could I yell, 'Grab the tiller a sec while I do this' or 'I feel ever so hungry!?' or the beautiful, 'It's your turn to steer!' Once again I was relying 100 per cent on my own ability to push my yacht around the world. It has its satisfactions—but also its drawbacks.

As I approached the narrowest section of the Bali strait, I could see a tremendous current creating huge breaking waves and moved in very close to the Bali coast looking for calm water. At my first attempt I was not close enough and got swept back out, almost as fast as I could blink. At the second attempt, I got so close to the shore it looked certain that I would hit the reef—but I was still plucked up by the current and swept back out. Each time I had been forced backwards, with a bemused expression on my face, I had passed a local fisherman who sat a couple of yards offshore in his dinghy. The first time I passed him, going backwards, he smiled; the second time he burst out laughing and beckoned me over, indicating he was willing to help. We tied his dinghy behind Shrimpy and set off into the strait for the third time, my pilot steering Shrimpy so close to the shore reef, I closed my eyes, but we got through and he left me to go on my way with a wave of bon voyage.

I reached the north coast of Java without further incident and sailed slowly westwards along it. Discovering that my visa was about to expire, I stopped at a small port to renew it and was told I had to make a four-hour journey inland to Jember to do so! I set off by Bemo early the next day and arrived in Jember at about three in the afternoon. Thinking the quickest way to find the immigration office was to hire a 'trishaw' proved a big mistake. Before moving off my 'driver' assured me he knew the place but, by the second circuit of town, I was beginning to have my doubts. I eventually found the place not 20 yards from where I first got into the 'trishaw', but it was shut. After much persuasion, I got them to stamp my passport, but then found that the price was more than I had with me! Getting back to Shrimpy around midnight, I had to go through the whole rigmarole again the next day. At least this time I knew where the office was!

A day or so further along the coast, I arrived at Jakarta—the capital of Indonesia—yeuch! After the green mountains and blue seas of most of Indonesia, Jakarta was a real shock, passing through a huge unused fleet of oil tankers moored off the land I sailed into the filthy port surrounded by seething humanity. Luckily I saw a small group of yachts in a little calm corner of the port and sneaked across there before the port authorities could spot me and shove me into the bumpy visiting yachts' mooring. Being Saturday, a couple of owners were on their yachts and watched with great interest as Shrimpy sailed up to them. One of the yachties was not only interested but astonished, for his yacht had also been built by Nobby Clark and the yachtie—Mike—had been told about Shrimpy when enquiring of his own yacht's sailing ability! Between them, these Western yachties, mainly American, made my stay in this horrible city a very pleasant one. They provided a 24-hour guard for Shrimpy, took me ashore, showed me around and partied me, even providing a car and chauffeur, so I could gather the stores I needed in comfort!

From Jakarta I sailed slowly northwards along the muddy, mangrove covered eastern coast of Sumatra, anchoring each night but not going ashore, as my sailing permit for Indonesia had now expired. Crossing the equator back into the northern hemisphere for the first time since the Galapagos islands, way back on the far side of the Pacific, I was hit by a very large thunderstorm, seemingly as a reminder not to get too cocky with King Neptune. I had to sit in the cockpit soaking wet and freezing cold all night doing my best to avoid the ever-increasing flow of cargo ships and oil tankers which gave proof I was reaching one of the busiest ports in the world—Singapore.

My last few days in Indonesia were spent wandering through the hundreds of tiny islands of the Archipelago of Riou, picking tiny shallow channels in order to keep out of the shipping. The final anchorage at the northernmost tip of the archipelago providing the great contrast of Indonesia's natural tropical swampiness and quiet evenings with the blazing lights and noise emanating from Singapore, the skyscrapers and neon signs of the city now only a stone's throw away, clearly visible on the horizon and blanketing out the stars.

Next morning, with sails up and engine flat out, I raced across the Singapore strait for, like the English Channel, its narrow, busy, current strewn waters are no place for a little yacht to linger. Quite soon I was in Singapore harbour, its waters rougher than the sea outside, churned around by countless small boats on various errands for their many big brothers at anchor in port. After a lot of searching and directions from two police launches, I finally found the customs dock for yachts in a tiny uncomfortable corner of the harbour.

Obtaining clearance was a cold, unfriendly and expensive business; the most costly part being for the inspection of Shrimpy and the issuing of a huge certificate stating I had no rats on board! I know this is standard practice for big ships, but never before in all the countries I had visited had little Shrimpy been asked for such a thing! I later met a man who came to question me about little-boat sailing, as he was going to attempt to voyage from Singapore to Australia by canoe. He was not allowed to leave without his deratification certificate! 'Red tape' is alive and well in Singapore!

Very happy to get away from the officials and out of the dirty bumpy main port, I had a choice of two yacht clubs, one with clean but bouncy moorings and the other with calm but dirty ones. I chose the latter and sailed around to the Republic of Singapore Yacht Club, where I was given a mooring for one week. I wanted to stay much longer but the mooring fees were exorbitant and on checking I found the other yacht club no cheaper, so it looked like my stay in Singapore was to be a very short one. But no, two committee members of the club—an English school teacher and a German importer, were very interested in Shrimpy's wanderings and persuaded the committee to give me a month's free moorings in exchange for an account of my voyage! I accepted this generous offer and the talk—which I gave in due course, with Shrimpy hauled out of the water and placed next to the club house for inspection—was quite a success. Many yacht club members turned up to listen, but with this—as with most of the club's activities—it was mainly the European members who took part. The motorboating Singaporians, who make up the majority of the membership, are willing to pay the high prices just to use the club as a parking place for their boats and are never seen in the club house from one year to the next.

Sadly, this very old, famous club seemed to be on its last legs and dying a painfully slow death. Its site—which must have been a gloriously calm quiet little backwater—is succumbing to the crowded, rapidly expanding, massive population of Singapore. A main drainage ditch had been led into the head of the creek and at low tide each day the flood gates were opened creating a massive current of crude sewage, garbage, etc, and I got quite used to having the odd dead pig bump Shrimpy on its way out to sea. Many tourists visiting Singapore get the impression of a very clean city, but that cleanliness is only 'main road' deep. The actual 'death blow' to the club will come quite soon when construction begins on the already planned low road bridge across the mouth of the creek—isolating the backwater from the sea.

Exploring the island, I found life very fast, noisy and crowded. The

high-rise flats which cover the land provide housing for the majority of
Singaporians and are the government's pride and joy, but their crude
interiors and money-saving absurdities, such as lifts which only stop
at every third floor, plus the high rents, made me shudder. Add to this
the racial tension—a mixture of Chinese, Indian and Malay, with quite
a few Europeans thrown in for good measure and you have a melting
pot which, while on the surface seems calm enough, is seething
beneath. My impression of Singapore was of a crowded noisy facade of
affluence on a fast trip to hell; an interesting place to visit but no place
to live.

Back in the relative calm of the yacht club, where the hum of distant
traffic was almost overcome by the buzzing of not distant enough
mosquitoes, I met the Captain of a very large, fast, racing yacht and he
invited me out for a sail to show me 'how a real yacht goes'. So, next
morning, loaded to the gunwales with food, booze and a crew of
yachties and local girls, this sleek machine slowly crept out of the
shallow creek. At the mouth of the creek we all helped get the sails up
and off she went at a blistering pace. I was very impressed, but not for
long because no more than half a mile out, the skipper had managed to
hit the first reef he came to and we spent the whole day aground at a
very uncomfortable angle waiting for the tide to refloat us, then we
motored slowly back home, but not before grounding once more, by
passing a buoy in the creek on the wrong side. So that's how a 'real
yacht goes' is it? I'll stick to Shrimpy thanks!

With many helpful friends, I used the club's facilities to clean and
prepare Shrimpy for the next leg of the voyage. The only really big job
was to replace two chain plates which had almost rusted through; I
managed to get them off without too much of a struggle and took them
to the boatbuilder who had his workshop in the yacht club grounds and
asked him to make two new ones for me in stainless steel—the exact
copy of the old ones. His first attempt was not very impressive, for
somehow he had managed to make the replicas upside down and back to
front! It must have been something to do with the famed 'mysterious
and devious oriental mind'—but eventually he managed to make
something which would work and, after I had fitted them, Shrimpy was
ready to go.

A quick trip down to the customs office in the main harbour to get
clearance—where officials were less than amused at the scene from the
Pied Piper I had drawn on the back of my deratification certificate. A
farewell drink at the yacht club with the many friends I had met there
and we were off—sailing northwards along the Malacca strait from the
noise and bustle of Singapore to the more tranquil coast of Malaya.

Sailing and motoring slowly along the coast of Malaysia in light
breezes and calm seas, I spent a few very leisurely days learning to relax

again after Singapore's mad whirl. The tensions and pressures of noise, polluted air and crowds soon left me, along with the permanent headache I have whenever I'm in a city. I sailed in the daytime and anchored each night, keeping in the shallow coastal waters which stretch many miles offshore—ensuring none of the big ships would be able to get near Shrimpy let alone hit her.

Eventually I arrived at the port of Malacca and went ashore to get clearance for Malaysia. It was nice to see 'human' officials again—in the form of a customs officer who burst out laughing when I flourished my Singaporian 'deratification certificate' and who, unlike Singapore's expensive red tape men, granted me clearance free of charge. I was a bit upset that all he gave me was a passport stamp which read: 'Malacca landing pass, valid during ship's stay in Port' but later discovered that this was all I needed for any Malaysian port, with absolutely no time limit! In the days I spent in Malacca, I found people living life happily at a relaxed pace—as, indeed, throughout Malaysia. Though almost penniless compared to their affluent Singapore neighbours, they have to my mind, a much richer life.

Further north from Malacca, I was approaching the maze of swampy mangrove islands which protect the harbour of Port Swettenham, when a sudden breeze quickly made the sea very choppy and uncomfortable. The wind was dead against me so I decided to turn shorewards to try and find a small passage into port rather than plod on to the main entrance. As I approached the shore I saw what appeared to be a tiny cargo ship pitching up and down to its anchor uncomfortably in a very exposed position. Wondering why he didn't chug into the calm waters of the swamp (many of the channels were more than adequate for him) and thinking he might have a problem, I altered course a few degrees in order to pass very close to him. By the time I was within half a mile, a tiny powerboat shot out from under his lee and charged straight at me. As it neared, I could see a man in uniform manning the machine gun on its bow! They motioned me to stay well away from the little cargo ship and stayed buzzing around me to make sure that I complied with their demands. When I finally reached the yacht club, where I was made very welcome indeed, I discovered that the little cargo ship was one of the first to be hi-jacked off the coast of Vietnam and, with its sad overflowing cargo of refugees, was being barred from entering port by worried, frustrated immigration officials. Throughout my three days stay in port I—and all the other yachties—were pressured by reporters to sail them to within speaking distance of the refugee boat but, like all reporters, they had very little money to spend and didn't realise just how much would be needed before a foreign yachtie would be prepared to risk official ire!

A few more days of light, easy sailing and Shrimpy entered the large beautiful estuary of Pangor and was soon anchored off the village's pretty little yacht club. Pangor Yacht Club consisted of about half a dozen yachts and a handful of members, mainly Europeans working in the large inland town of Ipoh and, despite the fact that they met only once a month for a weekend, the club was opened every day by the Malay couple who lived in it and showers, drinks and hot meals were available whenever I, or Doug, wanted. Doug was the only other visiting yachtie—an American with a beautiful ocean-going yacht. He was a very frustrated sailor, one of those who wants to do so much but whenever he puts his nose out of harbour gets into all sorts of problems. Doug was a radio ham, as are many American yachties, so soon all the yachts in the area knew where Shrimpy was.

When I arrived in port, Doug was in the process of rebuilding his engine, which had got wrecked on his previous passage. He was also waiting to be sent a crewman by a friend in Singapore. We became very friendly—helping each other with various odd jobs, then one day he rowed his dinghy out from the shore with a big grin on his face and two pretty young girls sitting in the stern—'How do you like the crew I've been sent?' he shouted. Unhappily, the problem of personality, the dreaded disease of many a small yacht, soon rose its head and, when I encountered the yacht after its next problem-strewn voyage, relationships among the three of them were at a very low ebb.

Sailing out of the Pangor estuary, I continued northwards towards Penang Island. When night fell, I closed the shore and anchored as usual; cooked supper, put the hurricane lamp up in the rigging, and went to bed. I was woken at four in the morning by the sound of water rushing past the hull and the anchor chain creaking and groaning under the strain. I had not thought there was so much current around here when I anchored the previous night and had only let out a bare minimum of chain to make things easier in the morning. Therefore, I forced myself fully awake and went on deck to let out some more chain for safety's sake. The current seemed to be screaming past— unbelievable! Looking around, I could see nothing. It was a pitch black moonless night. I noticed my light had gone out but didn't bother to relight it as dawn was only an hour away. Instead, I would sit in the cockpit and stay awake, making an early breakfast and ready for an early start. While I sat in a still, calm night, I thought I could vaguely hear the sound of engines in the distance but could see no lights. Just before dawn I saw early morning fires being lit ashore then—horror of horrors—I watched them pass Shrimpy at the same speed as the current! What was going on? As dawn broke all became apparent to me, for way ahead I could see two little trawlers on a parallel course and the trawl net slung between them had picked up my anchor chain when they passed each side of unlit Shrimpy during the night. Quite oblivious to the fact they were dragging me along behind them!

It was now daylight and I was shouting and waving, trying to catch the attention of the trawlers. When they eventually saw me they waved back pleasantly and indicated by signs that I should not sail between them—they thought I was catching them up under my own power! Eventually, I gave up trying to stop them and sat down for a free ride for they were going in the right direction. When at last they stopped to haul in their nets and saw me stop at the same time, understanding dawned and, with much good humour on both sides, we eventually got ourselves untangled and were relieved to find that no damage had been done to the trawl net. I explained the name of my yacht so that they could add to the number of fishermen's tall tales by telling everyone of the day they caught an 18-foot shrimp! And we parted friends. It was an amusing incident, but what if the sea had been rough? I had been planning to spend Christmas in Penang Island but when I reached it and discovered that the main harbour, though looking quite good on the chart, was a miserable place for a small yacht to anchor, I stayed only long enough to take on stores and was soon sailing north again, bound for Lang Kawi.

★ ★ ★

In the course of my voyage around the world, countless people have asked: 'Where is the most beautiful place?'. It's an impossible question to answer—I maintain that Utopia is constant movement coupled with complete freedom. Each place has some good and some bad, but as far as paradise goes, Lang Kawi Island has an awful lot of good and hardly any bad; it must be very near the top of the list. A perfect climate, calm blue seas, sandy bays and jungle green hills provide a wonderful backdrop for the handful of villages and the single hotel on an island which, happily, had not yet been 'discovered'. To add to the beauty, the main island is surrounded by hundreds of tiny ones, all hilly and most with pretty little beaches. It was just off one of these smaller islands that I met a very unusual sight as I sailed Shrimpy into the natural harbour. At first I thought it was a huge boatshed, curiously out of place on a tiny uninhabited island, but as I got nearer, I could see that it wasn't attached to the shore at all and was, in fact, a houseboat of unbelievable proportions! I sailed around it with my eyes popping out of my head. On its deck stood six assorted speed-boats (all bigger than *Super Shrimp*) and hanging in davits on each side were two 'Cigarette' power boats each capable of 75 miles per hour. The whole of the stern of the houseboat was an enormous bar and it was from here that the Captain hailed me with the words: 'Dinner's ready, tie up alongside!'

Later, with a four-course haute cuisine meal under my belt and the

139

crew of the houseboat generously doing my laundry and fixing my sick outboard, I was given a tour of the *Dari Laut* as the houseboat was named, which literally translated means 'of the sea'. The two owners, whom I later met, one English and one American, lived on board most of the time, each in his own flat on either side of the *Dari Laut* and each owning one of the fantastic 'Cigarette' power-racers. The other speedboats, plus skis, diving gear, fishing rods, etc, were available for use by up to nine paying guests who could be accommodated in beautiful cabins in air conditioned luxury. All in all, an amazing set up and judging from the number of local fishing boats circling it every night, the natives just couldn't believe their eyes! The friendly, generous owners of the houseboat allowed visiting yachts the use of their facilities and helped in many ways. Come Christmas, all the yachties in port which included myself and Doug, with his two girl crew—safely but uncomfortably arrived from Pangor—were invited aboard for an unbelievable eight-course Christmas dinner, followed by drinks and dancing in the huge bar with the Malay crew, the Australian mechanic, the American Captain and his stunningly beautiful Indian wife all joining in and making for me a very memorable night.

In a fairy-tale land like Lang Kawi such fairy tales are common; here's another example: A few days later I met two rather beautiful Australian girls at the little hotel on the main island and they told me a story of buried treasure on one of the smaller islands. They wanted to search for it but couldn't trust the local boats to keep their secret from official ears. I offered the services of *Super Shrimp* and, next day, we sailed. They seemed to know exactly which island and which beach—so I presumed they had a map, although I never saw it. Soon the boat was anchored in knee-deep water and we were off ashore, treasure-hunting! A romantic way to pass a day, you might say, but we actually found what we were looking for! One of the girls, Anne-Marie, suddenly gave a delightful shout and Debbie and I rushed to examine the find. I was amazed! Although our 'find' would probably be considered worthless by the big commercial outfits, I was stunned by the excitement of it all!

Despite pressure from all around me to whom I have told this story (including my publisher), I am not prepared to reveal any more about the type of treasure we found or even the island it was on, for stories such as this, about places such as this, must, in my opinion, remain tantalisingly evasive to all but those who are actually prepared to search. Who knows? Maybe we didn't find it at all!

In the wonderland of Lang Kawi, time had no meaning at all and living at its relaxed pace I had to keep reminding myself that the seasons wait for no man and it would soon be the right time to set out across the Indian Ocean. Before stocking up for my voyage to Sri Lanka, I decided to sail completely around the main island and, taking a friend with me, we set off on the three-day trip which involved sailing partly in Thailand's waters—as Lang Kawi is on the northern borderline of Malaya. We found many pretty little bays and stopped for a swim in the huge fresh water lake which takes up most of the space on the second largest island of the group. Arriving back at the main anchorage after a beautiful sail around this beautiful island, I dropped off my friend and took Shrimpy into town to buy stores. When I say I took Shrimpy into town, I quite literally mean it, for 'town' was a group of shops fronting on the main road and backing on to the sea and, at high tide, I could get Shrimpy to within 'provision-throwing' distance of the shops' back doors. I then waded ashore to order and pay for what I wanted, waded back to Shrimpy and had the shopkeeper throw me all my packages one by one out of his back door! A final sail over to *Dari Laut* to say farewell to my many friends on board and to be given presents of hot-toasted sandwiches and cold cans of beer, I was off to sea—the Indian Ocean awaited.

17

Across the Indian Ocean
January 3–March 25 1979

Leaving Lang Kawi behind and heading west once more, I was faced
with my first long single-handed sail since the Atlantic and it took quite
a while for me to come to terms with the fact but after a few days and a
few very rusty sun sights, I was back in tune with my little boat and the
big seas. The only obstacles between me and my next port in Sri Lanka
were the Nicobar Islands. These, along with their neighbours, the
Andamans, contain a mixture of hostile natives and indian prisoners
and I had heard many stories of yachts which had strayed too near
them, being attacked or shot at. I naturally kept well clear of the islands,
sailing just close enough to bring them over the horizon in order to
check my navigation.

The rest of the trip across the top of the Indian Ocean, or the bottom
of the Bay of Bengal (depending on which map you look at) took just
under two weeks. Two weeks of ideal sailing weather; indeed the
voyage was so perfect it is hard to describe. No gales, no calms and no
small dramas. Just a gentle wall of wind day and night pushing Shrimpy
serenely along through the low, even swell with small phosphorescent
wavelets lapping at the hull. It may not have been the weather for
racing sailors—that strange breed of competitive people who actually
enjoy life when the boat leans over ('heels' to them) but it was just right
for me. The only things I did on this trip which could be classed as
sailing, were to put up the running sail and set the self-steering at the
start of the voyage and to take the sail down again before hitting Sri
Lanka! Navigation was a bit more difficult for my route lay parallel to,
and only a few miles north of, the main shipping lane which was very
crowded and I had to ensure that I didn't drift too far south and get
trapped among the huge cargo ships. This proved no great problem,
but did mean that I had to take more sights—twice a day as opposed to
my usual, lazy once every two or three days and it cut deeply into my
leisure time. Time to do what? Well, mainly nothing and the
pleasantness of 'nothing' means sitting comfortably and quietly in the
cockpit watching the sea and the sky roll by. This, interspersed with
periods of great activity such as playing my little wooden flute for
visiting dolphins, preparing meals whenever I felt hungry and singing

142

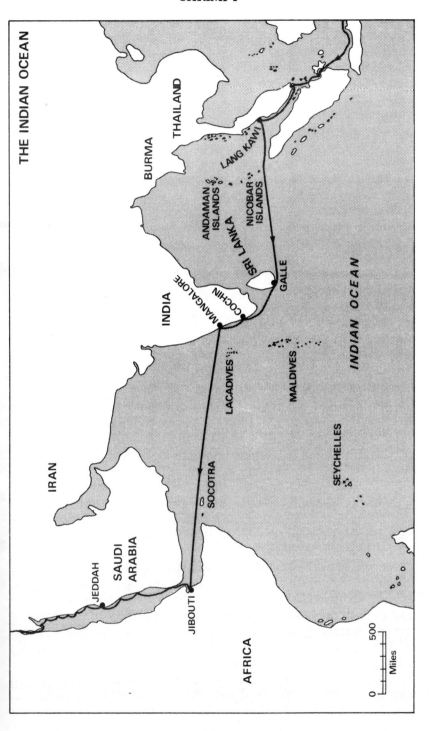

to the moon, made the days drift happily by.

At the end of the first week Shrimpy had reached the longitude of 90 degrees east which meant that she had now sailed three-quarters of the way around the world and I celebrated with my last can of *Dari Laut* beer! The end of a perfect sail has to have a perfect port, Galle, Sri Lanka, was just that. Flat, calm, well protected waters overlooked by an old Dutch fort and a pretty little town. Half a dozen travelling yachts at anchor, some of which were old friends and the others new people and, from the shore, shouts of welcome from happy smiling faces. Shrimpy was soon bobbing at her anchor, while I gave her a good look over and was very pleased to find that nothing whatsoever needed repairing or renewing after her long but gentle voyage from Malaya. Giving her a pat, I jumped into the dinghy and rowed ashore to get clearance from the customs. On offering around my cigarettes in the customs house, I was rewarded by an over-enthusiastic welcome and courteous, speedy service, which made me very suspicious, until they informed me that I had arrived in Sri Lanka in the midst of a tobacco manufacturer's strike and cigarettes ashore were only obtainable at expensive black market prices! As word got out that a new yacht carrying cigarettes had arrived, I was swamped by crowds of dock workers. Little did they know that I was on my last packet and would soon be joining their 'beedie' smoking ranks. 'Beedies' are a cheap, poor (very poor) local substitute for cigarettes, but are much better than nothing to nicotine addicts like me!

Before I could get on with my sightseeing, I had to pay a visit to Don Winsor who has a beautiful large old house just outside the port gates and whose name and address had been given to me by many yachts in many varied ports throughout the world. Don is one of the better known of that small select band of people who, while not being sailors themselves, take a great interest in the wanderings of small yachts, helping yachties find whatever they need at reasonable prices and generally providing hospitality in various harbours throughout the world. In return, they make many friends and meet many adventurers—both famous and infamous—but mainly, they get a much more worldly outlook on life than their neighbours.

Don was ideally situated for his hobby, as Port Galle is a main crossroads for cruising yachts and he provides showers, meals, post restante, accommodation, bicycle hire, etc. Being in the midst of all the flow of yachties' news and gossip, which is as lengthy and malicious as any housewives' 'garden fence' variety, Don had, naturally, heard about *Super Shrimp* long before I arrived and, trading him cigarettes for beer, as we sat chatting on his verandah, we soon became friends.

As I wandered around Galle and then wider afield, I was impressed with the beauty of the island and with the amazingly cheap cost of living—admittedly it didn't seem cheap for the locals who work for

Above *Snug anchorage in a mangrove swamp, North Queensland.* **Below** *Wash-day on the uninhabited coast of North Queensland.*

Left *Anchored off Cooktown, Australia.*

Below left *Goodbye Australia, Indonesia here we come.*

Right *My wonderment at the workmanship of an Indonesian dugout canoe is equalled only by their wonderment at the workmanship of our European inflatable dinghy!*

Below *Going to market, Lombok style.*

Below right *A beautiful cargo-carrying Indonesian yacht slips slowly and silently past us in light airs.*

Above *Shrimpy arrives in the perfectly protected harbour of Galle, Sri Lanka and I row ashore in the dinghy.* **Below** *Shrimpy battles manfully through the Red Sea.*

pitiful wages, but it must be the ideal place for a low budget holiday, or even retirement, as was borne out by the number of Europeans wandering around wearing huge rucksacks. The best way to travel any distance was by train, but I discovered that you had to be very fast, very sly or very strong to get a seat.

Whilst getting Shrimpy stored up for the short hop across to India, I had a happy surprise. Two of Iris' friends arrived from Switzerland carrying a big parcel full of goodies which she had made up for me. I spent a few days with them and took them out for a short sail on Shrimpy, but, despite their excellent company, the package plus all the news from Iris which they had brought me, made me very impatient to be off and soon Shrimpy was merrily bobbing across the Gulf of Mannar.

Only two days out from Port Galle, and I sighted Cape Comorin the southernmost tip of India. My intention was to sail northwards along the western coast of India before heading out across the Sea of Oman, in order to get the prevailing winds dead aft for this longish leg to the entrance of the Red Sea. I was hoping for good weather, as there are very few decent harbours along the coastline and the swell is usually quite rough. The gods were kind and I was able to sail in perfect safety quite close to the huge breakers which crashed unceasingly along the straight, sandy Indian coastline. At frequent and regularly spaced intervals, I would pass a small village of mud huts dominated by huge stone churches and the terrible poverty of southern India was apparent even from my restricted viewpoint. With no shipping and no offlying rocks, the only navigational hazard was the fleets of fishing canoes. These consisted of three or four balsa-wood tree trunks lashed together and each evening, thousands would be launched through the large surf by the one-man crews with their clothing, smokes, etc, tied on their heads, off to sit fishing all through the night. Only the most skillful would get a dry evening! The only lights they had were wooden torches, which would be lit as Shrimpy approached them and quickly extinguished when she had passed. The night was filled with astonished voices as the fisherman near enough to Shrimpy's course to see her, shouted her description to those further away—I wish I could have understood just what they were saying!

I reached the port of Cochin and, after quite a battle against a strong outgoing current in the long narrow entrance channel, I succeeded in getting into the calm waters of the harbour. Cochin is a very busy port and as it was already dusk, I decided to anchor for the night on a shallow patch where no big ship could plough into me. This being accomplished, I was soon happily asleep.

Next morning, I found the customs jetty and went ashore to get clearance. Straight away I ran into a problem. The officials were not used to small visiting yachts and, although very polite and correct, informed me that the minimum port charge was really scaled for cargo ships and I already owed them some astronomical figure for my overnight stay! Although they all readily agreed that it was an absurd sum for little Shrimpy, they refused to bend the rules until, after a whole two days of filling in forms and getting shoved from office to office, I eventually found a high official who had enough humanity to overcome his officialdom and convert my charges to a reasonable figure.

As soon as I had finished the entry formalities, I turned round and went straight back through all the offices in reverse order making my exit papers, pausing only long enough to buy a few packets of cigarettes and a bit of food from a nearby stall, I jumped aboard Shrimpy and sailed hastily away from Port Cochin's jumble of red tape.

Continuing northwards along the coast, I decided my next port would have to be a much smaller one and, for this reason, I was soon entering the shallow Mangalore river port, in company with a fleet of local fishing boats who showed me the entrance channel. I was happy to find that there were no officials to bother me and no charges to pay in this pretty little port—which is closed for six months of the year when the weather makes its entrance impossible. It was, of course, no coincidence that I was sailing along this coast at the most favourable time of year. For, as in all other parts of the voyage, I had spent much time in planning my route, poring over the excellent pilot charts of the world, which show the wind direction and strength, prevailing currents, hurricane tracks and tons of other useful information, all gathered by— often bitter—experience of the many ships of bygone days. There must have been many times in the voyages of Captain Cook and his contemporaries when they would have given the earth to posses such knowledge as one pilot chart contains!

I moored Shrimpy alongside the jetty long enough to purchase and stow all the provisions I needed for the next ocean passage but the constant bumping and jostling of the hundreds of fishing boats plus the huge ever-growing crowd of spectators soon forced me to a calmer spot. I anchored in the centre of the river and began preparing Shrimpy for another long sail. Whilst hard at work, I was hailed by a passing canoe— one of the fleet of cross-river ferry boats—and saw that its passenger was a European. As the canoe sailed past, he invited me to up anchor and move Shrimpy over to where his yacht was moored as it was an ideal spot. 'Just follow us', he shouted. The local sailing canoes were much faster than Shrimpy but the skipper kept spilling wind, allowing me to keep pace and pointing out the shallow patches as we meandered up a pretty little sandy creek. It was so shallow that even Shrimpy could barely make it and I was beginning to wonder if I had heard correctly when, rounding the final bend, a huge yacht came into view. It was no

ordinary yacht, but a Wharram type catamaran almost 50 feet long—
these huge 'hairy' beasts have no more draught than Shrimpy!

I was soon tied up alongside and listening to an amazing tale. The
owner had built his yacht here, having discovered on a previous hitch-
hiking trip of the area, how amazingly cheaply such a project could be
carried out. The yacht had just been finished and the pricing had proved
correct but the problem was that the taxes, fees and bribes needed to
obtain clearance from customs to import things like sails, compass, etc,
had turned a cheap project into a very dear one and the owner was just
about bankrupt. He was not daunted, however, and was still full of
enthusiasm to set sail. I spent three days with him as I prepared
Shrimpy for sea and we became great friends. I later learnt that he set
sail not long after me, with the bare minimum of stores and had safely
reached Jibouti—but those Wharram cats are so fast he could be
anywhere by now!

★   ★   ★

Saying goodbye to India, I vowed to return someday, for I had not seen
nearly enough of this huge fascinating land but it was high time to set
out across the Arabian Sea because this treacherous corner of the Indian
Ocean has a very short favourable season.

The 28-day voyage across the Arabian Sea from Mangalore to Jibouti,
French Somaliland, proved to be calm and easy, but very slow going.
Not at all boring, however, for when the sea is oily calm it's amazing
just how much life there is to watch, from the enormous but gentle
whales, which always scare me to death just by looking at their sheer
bulk, right down to the many tiny little insects which scoot over the
surface of the sea hundreds of miles from land. Dolphins, of course,
provide the best entertainment, leaping tirelessly across the oceans in
simple but complete happiness. On a pitch black night, when all you
can hear is their breathing—which sounds like a bicycle-tyre
puncturing—and all you can see is their sparkling con-trails of
phosphorescence slicing across the sea at incredible speeds; it is a
wonderful experience.

Another pastime which never fails to interest and amuse me, is to
watch the tiny pilot fish that live under Shrimpy for protection, darting
out at anything drifting past that looks edible. How they can keep up
with the boat day after day and still find time to sleep, is a mystery to
me. Having kept well away from the shipping routes, the sea was mine
alone for the first 25 days, but with about 100 miles to go, I saw another
yacht appear over the horizon behind me. This was the first time I had
seen another yacht at sea since I started sailing seven years ago, so it was
quite an event. He gradually overhauled me and as he passed he slowed

down to have a chat; the language was no problem as he had sailed from Southampton! The catamaran was called *Peptide*.

Nearing Jibouti, the lumps of oil I had seen floating on the surface ever since I had entered the Gulf of Aden, got denser and denser until, on dropping anchor off the yacht club, it was a solid mass.

Among the dozen or so visiting yachts, I was happy to see some old friends. Everyone was getting ready to attack the contrary winds of the Red Sea and were busily exchanging ideas as to which of the ports in this troubled part of the world would be safe to enter, without being shot at. One big motorboat already had a huge bullet hole in its side because the skipper had got too close to one of the islands off Socotra and had been shot at on sight.

The town of Jibouti was dirty, hot, drab and fearfully expensive. The surrounding countryside was just as depressing. If it hadn't been for the friendliness and hospitality of the local yacht club, Jibouti would have been unbearable. The club provided me with all my needs and more— water, showers, booze, meals, and its members were as helpful and friendly as I could wish for.

Eventually Shrimpy was fully stored and ready to go, but was I? The pilot charts told a terrible tale of the Red Sea: 95 per cent contrary winds, lack of shelter, dangerous reefs, wayward currents, mirage effects making navigation hazardous and sextant sights unreliable, extremes of temperature, and so on. Many yachts much bigger than Shrimpy had tried and failed, many of the larger yachts anchored around me were apprehensive of their own chances, let alone Shrimpy's. I knew this was going to be the hardest part of the voyage but I had faith in my brave little boat and, by now, I had a little experience of how to sail her. I also had an enormous incentive—Iris was waiting for me in the Mediterranean.

Come on then Shrimpy, let's give it a try . . .

18

Batterings in the Red Sea
March 25–May 15 1979

About a day's sail from Jibouti saw Shrimpy entering the Red Sea through the very narrow and terrifyingly busy straits of Bab-el-Mandab. Happily, the sea was calm and the breeze good, so I managed to avoid all the shipping without getting too many more grey hairs. It was a pitch-black night so I was sailing without lights! This may sound stupid and highly illegal but when in 'one-way' shipping lanes where all the big boats are travelling in the same direction, I prefer that they don't know of my existence, for then I can be fairly sure that they won't make any sudden course changes and I can more easily stay out of their way.

As the straits disappeared behind me and the Red Sea widened out, I was soon able to get away from the shipping lanes, put up a light, set the self-steering and go to bed. The next morning I awoke to find a horrible looking sky waiting for me and slowly but surely the wind steadily built up to a full southerly gale. The combination of strong winds and the short steep waves of the Red Sea, gave me a very uncomfortable time and, worst of all, it was completely dunking the outboard every few seconds.

Time to seek shelter, so I headed for the barren volcanic peaks of uninhabited Hanish Island. The last two miles before I could reach the lee of the island was very hairy, as it involved sailing beam on to the wind and the waves and one extra large wave broke on to the mainsail and ripped it open. As I struggled into the calm, protected waters of a leeward bay, my sails in tatters and the outboard too wet to work, a wonderful surprise was waiting for me. For there sat a big, red boat which I had already met in Jibouti, with a group of French scuba divers on board. So, instead of having to wait out the gale by myself, I had good company, cold wine and cheese, all the fish I could eat and an opportunity to borrow scuba gear to examine the fantastic underwater world of the Red Sea reefs. By the time the gale had abated, I had mended the mainsail, dried out the engine and got it working again, been given addresses and good wishes by my new found friends and was ready to go.

Another week of sailing by day and anchoring each night got me through the tricky maze of coral reefs and islands off the North Yemen coast and into the brand new Port of Jizan in Saudi Arabia. In most parts of the world it's a great pleasure to get off the sea for a while, but in Jizan—as all other places along the Saudi coast—all you are doing by going ashore is moving from a desert of water to a desert of sand. With modern plumbing and air conditioning, however, it is possible to make your own self-contained oasis anywhere on earth and in Jizan it was a group of French port constructors who had done just this and I spent three gloriously cool days with them!

Shrimpy was the first yacht to sail into this brand new port—built for offloading cargoes of cement and already ankle deep in the stuff (lucky it never rains there!). The officials didn't know what to do with me, but eventually, with help from the French, all my papers were found to be in order and I was allowed the freedom of the port. I was not at all impressed by it and was soon sailing onwards along the barren reefy coastline of Saudi, having to stop every night for fear of hitting a reef in the dark. I was making painfully slow progress for I had now reached the part of the Red Sea where the wind blows continually from the north all year round, and usually quite strongly, but eventually I reached the port of Jeddah.

Having no large-scale chart of this huge and rapidly expanding dusty hot mass of blinding white concrete that is Jeddah—Saudi's main port both for produce and pilgrims (Mecca being a few hours inland), it took me quite a while to find a decent place to park Shrimpy. Eventually I found a large group of barges on which a German salvage company live and work. After having got permission, I tied up alongside and, as the complex of barges extended to the shore, I didn't even have to put my dinghy into the oily port waters.

The Germans were very friendly and helpful and I was washed and dined and driven around town in the company car to purchase all my provisions. When I got round to buying petrol for the outboard, the price for my requirement of 20 litres was so small that the garage attendant gave it to me for free rather than try to gather enough small change for my already small note!

Wandering around town, I discovered many strange sights, for the lifestyle of the average Saudi in this country which has got too rich too fast, is that of a kid in a candy store: people sleeping on the streets but watching colour TV plugged into a handy street lamp. Any new gadget which breaks down is thrown away for lack of repair facilities or knowledge and a new one immediately bought. Empty cans or packaging are just dumped anywhere you happen to be standing when you no longer need them. The thing that upset me most, however, was the complete ignorance of the average Saudi of anything foreign, brought about by years of censorship—for example, the customs officer who refused absolutely to believe I had no alcohol aboard my boat, for

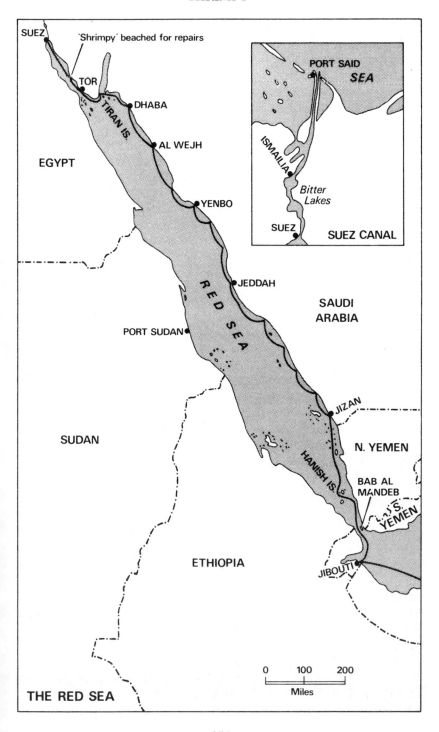

SUEZ

'Shrimpy' beached for repairs

TOR

DHABA

TIRAN IS.

AL WEJH

EGYPT

YENBO

PORT SAID

SEA

ISMAILIA

Bitter
Lakes

SUEZ

SUEZ CANAL

JEDDAH

SAUDI
ARABIA

PORT SUDAN

R E D   S E A

JIZAN

SUDAN

N. YEMEN

HANISH IS.

BAB AL
MANDEB

S.
YEMEN

ETHIOPIA

JIBOUTI

0   100   200

Miles

THE RED SEA

155

he was quite certain that it was impossible for a non-Moslem to exist without a daily bottle!

Sitting in Jeddah, halfway up the too hot, too dry, barren coast of the Red Sea, I could feel the Mediterranean beckoning me with great force. As I was preparing Shrimpy to leave and continue bashing into the constant head winds, a sandstorm hit the port so I postponed departure. I was very glad that I did, for this—the first sandstorm I had experienced—was an awe-inspiring thing. Hot, dry winds, gusting up to 60 knots, severely tested all the boats in the harbour and the sand and dust cut visibility down to less than 50 yards. Three days it lasted and, during that time, I had to leave all Shrimpy's hatches open, for it was much too hot to shut them. By the time the storm ended the whole boat inside and out was ankle deep in sand. All the meals I cooked tasted as gritty as a picnic on Blackpool beach and the dryness of the air made my skin so scaley I felt like a landed fish.

When all the commotion in the port had subsided and all the recent wrecks had been dragged away from the entrance to the harbour, it was time for Shrimpy to get underway—but not alone! While the storm was raging, I had become friendly with Jean-Claude and Crystal, who were sailing in an eight-metre French yacht called *Africa Kelt* and had sailed in just minutes before the sandstorm began. Communicating in a mixture of basic French and English and much more fluent sign language, we decided to sail together—for we were heading the same way. Although their little yacht (an enormous palace compared to *Super Shrimp*) was a fair bit faster, they were in no particular hurry.

As we sailed and motored northwards along the coast averaging about 25 miles a day and anchoring among the reefs each night, we found it very hard going, for the area is vaguely charted and it was necessary to navigate entirely by eye. We had to concentrate very hard all the time because a reef can crop up quicker than you can stop a yacht and it is very solid stuff to hit!

Our decision to sail together was soon rewarded as Shrimpy's engine broke down in a very dangerous area of reefs and *Africa Kelt* managed to tow me out before I hit anything. Later the same day, I was able to return the favour because, as we were approaching shallow water for the night's anchorage, the French boat grounded and got well and truly stuck on a sandbank. There was quite a swell running and she was bouncing viciously, but, luckily, Shrimpy with her shallow draught could fuss around her without touching the bottom and I was soon engaged in laying out anchors and lines in an attempt to pull *Africa Kelt* out of trouble. While we were all busily engaged in this task we saw a craft from a village nearby racing towards us full of people—help is on its way we thought. Not so. It turned out to be the local police force, who demanded we stop whatever we were doing while they inspected our papers and searched our boats!

For Jean-Claude, frantically working to save his boat, this was the last straw. I couldn't make out what he said to them or in which language—as he couldn't speak Arabic—but his meaning must have been crystal clear, for they left very quickly and we never saw them again! Eventually we managed to refloat *Africa Kelt* and anchored for the night.

A few days later we arrived at the port of Yenbo, an uninspiring place where everything looked half built or half derelict, the norm in Saudi. Despite the strict security regulations imposed on us: no visitors allowed on the yachts, or even allowed anywhere near them, being searched each time we left the port, being kept constantly under observation, etc, our three day stay in port was made very pleasant by a small group of English families. They lived in their own little fenced-in village on the outskirts of town, while working on various building projects. They gave us free use of their bathrooms and swimming pool—both fresh water—and fed and feted us. They also gave us T-shirts of the 'Yenbo Yacht Club' which consisted of two dinghies and a wind-surfer!

All across Saudi Arabia, small European communities such as this live in their own little villages working on various contracts. Admittedly the money they earn is very good, but how they can put up with the severely restricted life beats me, especially the women in a country where the female half of humanity is treated like dirt.

After a final party with our English friends it was with trepidation that we approached the immigration official's office to collect our departure permits, for we were very late—having promised to be there by six pm; it was now past ten. We found the office open and the official patiently waiting. Instead of his wrath, he gave us huge smiles, handshakes of bon voyage and loaded us up with packets of cigarettes.

Two days out of Yenbo, Shrimpy's engine packed up completely and *Africa Kelt* once again took her under tow. After spending two whole days searching for a passage through the reefs, we eventually arrived at the small port of Al Wejh. Our arrival caused quite a commotion, mainly because of the language barrier. Thinking it less complicated, official-wise for Shrimpy to enter port under her own steam, the plan was that Jean-Claude would cast Shrimpy off a few miles out and I would sail in while *Africa Kelt* continued under power. Everything went smoothly until, with the French yacht in port and beyond recall, the wind died completely and a strong current commenced to push Shrimpy away from harbour and back towards the reefs. There was nothing much I could do except switch on the radio to listen to the Cup Final, while I drifted around in a rather precarious position. It was much too deep to anchor and darkness—that much-feared enemy of coral reef navigation—was rapidly approaching.

Jean-Claude, excellent sailor that he is, had realised my predicament and, although he had by this time already made out his entry papers, set off to come and tow me in. He could not explain what he was about to the coastguard because they could not understand him and did not yet know of Shrimpy's existence, so they naturally assumed that something very fishy was going on and chased after *Africa Kelt* in their speedboat. You can imagine my surprise when, on hearing the noise of motors, I looked out of the cabin to see *Africa Kelt* charging full power on a very erratic course towards me with a little speed boat doing her utmost to head the yacht back into port! Eventually the coastguard (on seeing poor little becalmed Shrimpy) understood what was happening and allowed Jean-Claude to proceed with his rescue operation, but on reaching port another obstacle awaited us. A large cargo ship had arrived to unload cement—which, judging by the amount of the stuff that I had already seen in other ports, must be Saudi Arabia's staple diet! The ship had floating mooring ropes laid out all across the harbour to keep it off the reefs, so we anchored well away from this dangerous floating spider's web, just inside the harbour entrance. The little coastguard boat, however, wanted us where they could keep an eye on us until the big bosses arrived next morning, and they therefore demanded that we follow them. They, of course,were used to crossing over all the floating ropes in port with their speed boat's flat, shallow bottom and could not understand our refusal to follow them—for never before had they seen a small yacht with a deep keel. After much argument, they left us at anchor for the night. Next day, with the arrival of an English-speaking official, all was explained and tempers soothed.

When they learned of our valid reasons for all that had happened the previous night they became so generous and helpful it was unbelievable and the government mechanic soon had my little outboard running again along with a supply of spare plugs and oil—all for free. Within the confines of the tight security restrictions they did all they could to try to understand our needs and to help us; so much so that we managed to put up with the 'no visitors' rule and the armed guard detailed to dog our footsteps around town, without too much protest. Whenever I got vexed with the tight security and the—to my way of thinking—strange laws and customs of Saudi Arabia, it was very easy to calm myself down by thinking what would happen to a non-English-speaking Arab if he arrived by small yacht in a little English port. I remember also my Polish friend who arrived single-handed at Dover with a broken arm, in great pain, and was not allowed ashore for two days.

Leaving Al Wejh, we continued northwards and, as we neared the top of the Red Sea, we tried for greater and greater daily distances between our anchorages. *Africa Kelt* would slowly pull ahead of Shrimpy

looking for a likely spot to anchor while the sun was still high enough
to see the reefs, then an hour or so later, Shrimpy would arrive in the
gloom, guided by *Africa Kelt*'s position.

At Dhaba, a tiny village and port, but by far the most beautiful spot I
had seen along the whole coast of Saudi Arabia, we met another group
of English who pressed so many goodies on us we had to borrow their
truck to get it all down to the yachts!

About 30 miles north of Dhaba and just after noon, the wind
suddenly turned 180 degrees which, in this part of the world usually
means a storm is on the way. Jean-Claude turned south heading for a
nearby bay—but I was determined not to lose any ground so near to the
Gulf of Suez and continued northwards looking for less well-defined
shelter. Happily the storm did not materialise but, rounding Ras Wadi
Tiryam, I was signalled ashore by the coastguard and forced at
gunpoint to stay a whole day there while they checked my papers with
the nearest town by radio. All the time I was waiting at this guardpost, I
was very apprehensive for the soldiers here were pure desert tribesmen,
very ignorant of the outside world, only 60 miles from Israeli-held Sinai
and armed to the teeth! I had heard that with desert tribes a guest, even
an enemy, is sacred while in your camp so, after they had provided me
with cigarettes and a meal, I decided to test this legend. Walking up to
one of the guards on duty I asked in sign language if I could look at his
rifle; he was the only one with a gun actually to hand, no one else
moved but all were watching very intently. To my surprise, the guard
handed me his rifle! I removed the magazine to verify it was loaded,
replaced it, cocked the rifle, aimed it at a distant tree and put off the
safety catch. Everyone had stopped breathing but still no one moved. I
put the safety catch back on, uncocked the gun and handed it back to
the guard—gesturing what a nice weapon it was. Everyone breathed a
great sigh of relief—perhaps mine was the largest—yes, customs in
Saudi are different from England!

My papers verified, I left the coast of Saudi heading westwards under
the lee of a line of islands toward the Sinai peninsula. As I tucked
Shrimpy in among the reefs of Barqan island, anchoring for the night, a
speedboat from the Saudi coastguard station on the island came haring
out to see me and demanded that I sailed Shrimpy ashore. We spent a
lot of time arguing whether or not it was too dark to find the passage
through the reefs and, by the time they agreed to leave me where I was
for the night, it was pitch black. For the next hour I had the hilarious
entertainment of listening to a slowly receding engine, interrupted at
very frequent intervals by a solid crunching and much swearing as the
speedboat crashed its way from coral-head to coral-head in the general
direction of the island!

I left at the crack of dawn next day, having no intention of sitting around in a guardpost for another 24 hours and was relieved when I saw that no little speedboats had followed me.

Approaching Tiran island in the afternoon, I saw a very fast patrol boat steaming towards me. As it skidded to a halt just behind Shrimpy, I could see an Israeli flag waving at its stern. We had a long chat and they advised me not to go ashore on Tiran but allowed me to anchor there overnight. Then they sped off to resume their border patrol. I later discovered that this had been one of the three patrol boats which the Israelis, with their usual military flair, had pinched from a French port.

19

Shipwrecked
May 15–July 14 1979

Leaving Saudi Arabia and arriving at El'At in Israeli-held Sinai was like a trip in a time machine from the middle-ages to the present day and, on going ashore, I suffered from culture shock. It was beautiful to see once more the female half of humanity represented by bikini-clad flesh rather than the rare miscellaneous black blobs who wander around Saudi, and to find people who were able to talk of the world as a whole, rather than the ignorance of all things foreign that Saudi censorship has brought its people.

About an hour after I had arrived at El'At, *Africa Kelt* sailed into port. She had developed engine trouble and, finding no parts in El'At, she soon left again on a short trip down the coast to the military port of Sharm el Sheikh. Not a few hours later, however, she was back anchored next to Shrimpy in company with a tug boat; Jean-Claude explained that they had not been allowed even to enter the military harbour and all hell had broken loose when they were seen heading for it—the tug had been despatched to tow them back to El'At.

Having been assured that my help was not required to fix *Africa Kelt*'s motor, I set sail and soon rounded Ras Muhammad to leave the Red Sea behind me and commence my attack on the 150-mile long Gulf of Suez. The constant head winds of the Red Sea increased to head gales aided by the 'venturi' effect of the awe-inspiring barren mountains on each side of the gulf. Shrimpy, playing at submarines most of the time, was hard put crashing into the high, short, steep waves but gamely, mile by mile, we made our painfully slow progress towards the Suez Canal, delicately picking a route to avoid reefs, shipping lanes and minefields! Fortunately, there were enough protected anchorages to enable me to get a good sleep each night.

About ten miles north of Tor, the only port on the eastern side of the Gulf of Suez, an extra large rogue wave suddenly reared before me. Shrimpy climbed manfully to the top of it but then it abruptly collapsed and we fell about three metres through the air, to hit the surface of the sea with a tremendous crash. Minutes later, when I went into the cabin to get a cigarette, I was aghast to see the carpets floating in six inches of water! We were sinking fast; it was time to start inflating the dinghy—

but no—how could I desert my brave little craft after she had done so much for me? I was determined to fight.

I pointed Shrimpy shorewards and shook the reefs out of the sails, turned the outboard to full speed, grabbed a bucket and began baling like hell. The water continued to enter the boat faster than I could get rid of it and my hope was that I could ground Shrimpy before she sank. It was a desperately close thing but we made it and eventually were sitting on the beach at a crazy angle and getting thumped every minute by the breaking surf. When the tide receded, I was able to get all the water out of Shrimpy and have a good look at the leak. The plywood had a split about a foot long, but happily it was not at a joint. Having no glue on board which would set quickly enough before the tide returned, I blocked the hole with grease-covered bedding held in place by sawn up bits of furniture, used as wedges.

Anxiously I waited to see what would happen when Shrimpy floated again. While I was waiting for the tide to return, I saw a jeep coming across the desert towards me and, when it was a hundred yards away, it stopped. A young Israeli soldier stepped out and, with his gun pointed at me, he started forward. I walked over to meet him but he demanded I stop 20 yards away from him and asked me what I was doing there. I explained that my yacht was holed and that I was trying to effect repairs. He demanded to see my papers, which I got for him—his rifle barrel never wavering from my stomach. When he was satisfied that I was not dangerous, he handed back my papers, walked slowly backwards to his jeep, got in and sped off. I was astounded—there I was in the middle of desert with a big problem and the only other human in sight offered not a word of sympathy, not an inkling of aid, nothing!

When Shrimpy floated again, I was happy to find that my temporary repair did not leak at all. The sea was still rough so I carefully nursed Shrimpy northwards, my guts wrenching at each thump of her hull—but we were winning and, after what seemed like an age, my tired salt-encrusted eyes made out the lights of port Suez and soon we were sitting at anchor in calm oily water just outside the entrance to the canal.

As I sailed into port the next morning, I knew I faced quite a struggle to convince the Suez Canal authorities of Shrimpy's ability to make the passage through the Canal. Apart from lacking much of the safety equipment that yachts are required to carry, the main objection was that Shrimpy's five-horsepower Yamaha could not push her along at the required minimum speed of seven knots. While I was pondering on this, events soon fell into place enabling me to start off through the Canal the very next day! Firstly, I was introduced to the Prince of the Red Sea, a yacht agent with a reputation as varied as the fees he charged! He took me under his wing and managed to steer me through all the paperwork and official blind-eyeing required to obtain Shrimpy's transit papers, even to a farcical 'inspection' of my power unit, fire-fighting gear (I showed them a large bucket), bilge-pumps (the same large bucket), etc. The official charges of £35 plus the Prince's fee, £10, was not too bad a price to pay, but did not compare very favourably with the 75p that the Panama Canal had cost. It also meant that I was once again penniless, my Australian 'fortune' having finally been exhausted.

While the Prince was busily bustling me around from office to office, he received news of another yacht's arrival, so we bundled into his car and sped off to meet it. It turned out to be *Peptide*—the English catamaran I had met at sea outside Jibouti! We were very pleased to see each other again and Simon offered me a tow through the Canal, plus the use of a more powerful outboard motor which he had, lashed on *Peptide*'s deck. We were told that yacht towing yacht was not allowed, but decided to set off together anyway and see what happened. Next morning the pilots for *Peptide* and *Super Shrimp* arrived and it was easy to see which pilot was mine by the look of terror on his face when he saw the size of Shrimpy. Just before we set off, *Africa Kelt* arrived in port and I hastily told Jean-Claude and Crystal that I would wait in Port Said, at the other end of the Canal, for a chat with them.

The Suez Canal is just under a hundred miles long; it has no locks and very little current; in the middle of the Canal's length are two small lakes and on the banks of the smaller stands the beautiful little town of Ismailia. Yachts transiting the Canal stop overnight at Ismailia where they drop off the Port Suez pilots and pick up Port Said pilots for the second leg. The only problems for transiting yachts are the pilots that they are provided with! These people know very little of navigation and spend all their time asking for cigarettes, whisky and 'backsheesh'—my pilot was no exception, but Shrimpy soon managed to shut him up when we reached the first lake, for a headwind had sprung up creating large enough wavelets to soak the cockpit every two or three minutes. He quickly got fed up with constant drenchings and disappeared into the cabin, which was fine by me, for I knew where I was going better than he did and I would no longer have to listen to his constant begging. Five minutes later, however, he emerged with a very green face and spent the rest of the trip leaning over the side of the boat! As soon as we arrived at Ismailia, he disappeared before I had even finished tying Shrimpy up!

Only one pilot turned up at Ismalia for the second leg of the transit and he said that it would be permitted for *Peptide*—with him on board—to tow Shrimpy the rest of the way. He was in a great hurry, so soon we were off and charging full speed along the canal, *Peptide* dragging Shrimpy close behind her with both yachts' engines set at top speed. In this fashion we ripped along at about eight knots, watching the banks of the Canal—piled high with dredged up wreckage from the Egyptian-Israeli war—speed by. We were doing well until one of *Peptide*'s engines overheated and we had to slow down to a crawl for the final few miles to arrive at Port Said Yacht Club late at night. Many helpful hands were waiting at the jetty to take our mooring ropes and I was soon contentedly sleeping within sight of the Mediterranean.

Next morning, after paying my respects to Ali—who runs the extremely generous and helpful Port Said Yacht Club, I wandered ashore to look at the town and immediately fell in love with it. Port Said was nothing exceptional as far as towns go, but what attracted me to it was simply its good 'vibrations'—that undefinable 'something' very few places have which makes them seem to ooze contentment and peace—despite poverty, despite traffic noise and despite congestion.

Despite my happiness with the port, my friends on *Peptide* and *Africa Kelt*—who had arrived two days after us—I was very itchy to set sail, for Iris was ready to rejoin Shrimpy in the Greek Islands and I could hardly wait to see her again. I managed to scrounge together enough supplies for the trip to Cyprus, but the hole in Shrimpy's hull was another problem! I had not touched it since the first temporary repair I had made in the Red Sea! Although it was still only bunged up with greased bits of bedding material and wedges, not one drop of water had entered since I had refloated—so I decided not to touch it until I reached Cyprus; perhaps a rather foolhardy decision but having no money for slipping, screws and glue it seemed the easiest thing to do.

It was quite interesting sailing Shrimpy the few miles from Port Said Yacht Club to the Mediterranean, as the wind was against me and I had to tack to and fro across the busy canal—as I had no money to buy petrol for the outboard. I made it without hitting anything and as soon as possible set a course to take me out of the shipping lane. Faced with a long headwind sail to reach Cyprus, I resigned myself to the fact that I had to live constantly in the 'uphill' half of Shrimpy all the time, for when the self-steering is set and Shrimpy is leaning way over, ploughing through the waves, any shift of my weight from one side of the boat to the other, changes the course about 20 degrees! I could live in the 'downhill' side, which would be much easier and more comfortable, but it feels very unsafe psychologically and makes Shrimpy sail much less efficiently, which makes for slower passages. Living on the 'uphill' side means that muscles are constantly in use to stop my body sliding across the boat and makes a day's sitting very tiring—even when I have nothing to do. As for sleeping 'uphill': unlike most yachties who tie themselves into their bunks, I have developed, over the years, the ability to relax and sleep happily with an arm wedged into a shelf over the bed to stop me sliding around. In this way, should

Above *Idyllic isolated anchorages such as this one were few and far between as we sailed through the Greek isles.*

Right *Chugging slowly through the Canal du Midi.*

Left *We had about 150 locks such as this to negotiate . . .*

Below *. . . but each night we found a beautiful stretch of canal bank to moor to.*

Right *Back in home waters, tea time at Denver Sluice on the river Ouse.*

Below right *Shrimpy, almost lost among the 'normal' size boats of her escort, is welcomed home to Cambridge by hundreds of people lining the bridges and river banks.*

Below *The Mayor greets Shrimpy as she arrives back at the mooring she left eight years ago.*

Overleaf Super Shrimp *is put on display in Cambridge, to prove just how much can be done with such modest means, and that an adventure like ours is within anybody's grasp.*

an emergency happen, I can just release my arm and be thrown out of bed in seconds, rather than having to climb, half awake, over the rope and canvas web that 'uphill' snoozing yachties secure themselves with. (As for leaving a 'downhill' bunk in rapid time, you have to try it to realise just how difficult it is.)

I found the Mediterranean very cold after the bathroom temperature of the Red Sea, but it was a nice shade of blue, marred only by being covered with thousands of bits of floating plastic. I assumed this was because I was still not far away from Port Said with its busy shipping lanes—but no! I was to find that throughout this inland sea, famed for its clear, clean waters, I was never to be out of sight of bits of floating man-made debris consisting mainly of lumps of oil and plastic bags.

After about a week of uneventful sailing, I saw the island of Cyprus climb out of the sea ahead of me and I was soon moored in the snug but crowded yacht harbour at Larnaca. In the yacht marina, I first began a game with yachtsmen of the Mediterranean which provided me with great sport. It usually went something like this: A local yachtie, walking around the marina looking at all the yachts, would see tiny Shrimpy with her English flag flapping in the breeze, and stare at her with disbelief. He would then ask, 'Did you sail her all the way from England to the Mediterranean?' I would reply, 'Yes, the long way round'. 'Oh, you mean via Gibraltar instead of using the French canals?' 'No, I mean via the Atlantic, Panama, the Pacific, Australia, the Indian Ocean, Red Sea and the Suez Canal!' From this point the game would take many different turns. Many would walk hastily away from such an obvious liar. Others would laugh at a good joke and ask me to tell them honestly about the French canals. Some would be prepared to believe that Shrimpy could arrive via Gibraltar, but very few would accept that she had done exactly what I said she had. Word would spread like wildfire around the marina. A mad English yachtsman had arrived in an overgrown dinghy with fantasies he actually believed—and was not quenched until it reached someone who knew about Shrimpy's adventures!

During my first two days in Larnaca I didn't see much of the town because most of the time I walked around with my eyes to the ground looking for cigarette butts to smoke. Though broke in practice, I was again solvent in theory, for the *Cambridge Evening News* had sent me payment for some articles and I just had to wait until it reached me through Europe's slowly declining communications system. When the cash eventually arrived, I was able to get Shrimpy slipped and repair her hole with proper materials, which took a heavy load off my mind—despite the fact that the temporary repair had still not leaked a drop since the Red Sea. Her hull intact once more and shining with new paint, Shrimpy was placed back in the water and I was ready for off.

20

Tourist-tarnished Greece
July 14–August 1 1979

Just before I left Larnaca, Cyprus, a reporter came to interview me and, being very impressed with my story, wanted photos of *Super Shrimp* under sail. In order to achieve this he told me that he would sail out to meet me as I passed a little port along the coast. The weather, perfect when I left Larnaca, had deteriorated considerably by the time I was off this little port and the light was fading rapidly, when I saw a little sail appear ahead of me. Sure enough, the reporter had made his rendezvous—but whether he managed to get any decent photos would be hard to say, for as we bounced through the waves side by side like two wooden horses on a madly erratic merry-go-round, I could see him clutching camera in one hand and tiller in the other, trying desperately to steady himself for a shot.

As darkness fell, he turned back for port, while I continued westwards out across the Mediterranean towards the islands of Greece. The voyage was a slow, miserable affair, the variable winds and confused choppy seas of the Mediterranean were very uncomfortable compared to the long gentle swells and steady winds of the larger oceans. I was happy despite the terrible sailing conditions, for this leg of the voyage had a goal more important than any ordinary new lump of land; I knew that when I reached the island of Symi, Iris would be waiting there for me.

After ten days at sea—the last three spent in agonising calms, Symi rose on the horizon and soon I was sailing into the pretty little port. This picturesque village snuggling in the harsh hillside was spoilt only by the hordes of loud-mouthed unclothed tourists who, much to the annoyance of all but the cafe-owning locals, arrive by ferry each day. It meant nothing to me at all for there was no sign of Iris! While waiting for her to arrive and hoping she hadn't got lost or mistaken our rendezvous, I discovered with a jolt that I was back among the 'civilised' world with 'civilised' yachties and how terribly uncivilised they all seemed. Gone was the tranquility of the sea, the gentle, careful, helpful sailors who know how to respect their yachts and others, who moor with care and thought, who are happy to give and receive help and make life easy and comfortable for themselves and fellow sailors.

Here instead were the 'status' yachties who barge their boats around the sea exactly as they would their cars around a city. Bringing on holiday with them that well-developed herding instinct of city life and not even knowing how to relax, they are shocked and not a little afraid when a complete stranger smiles and says hello. After gouging through a fleet of already moored yachts and finding their main objective, an electricity point—more important than a bollard—they plug their boats into the land and sit, surrounded by useless electrical gadgets in bored solitary silence. The strange thing is that they actually appear to be enjoying themselves!

I was still waiting for Iris to turn up when a customs officer came to tell me that I had to sail to Rhodes to get papers before I could stay any longer in Symi so, after a few choice swear words about red tape, I set sail.

Rhodes was exactly as I expected it to be—a heaving mass of humanity fighting desperately to get a photograph of something that did not contain a fellow tourist. Rhodes must have been a beautiful place before it was 'discovered'. While waiting for my papers, a man with a very familiar face came to visit Shrimpy, but for the life of me I could not place him. He explained that he was a magician and I had probably seen him a few times on BBC TV many years ago. He was now working in Rhodes, but as it is forbidden to take money out of Greece, he had bought a little yacht with the idea of sailing around after his job was finished and would like to pick my brains. I happily answered his questions and inspected his tiny craft, offering what advice I could and thinking what a perfect profession he had to keep himself funded as he sailed from country to country!

By the time my papers were ready, the weather had deteriorated and strong winds were keeping all the 'small' charter yachts in port, but they didn't stop little 5½-metre Shrimpy from sailing and, after a wet, soggy night of freezing cold temperatures, I arrived back in Symi— there on the quay stood Iris!

In the days that followed, as I watched Iris and Shrimpy—the two women in my life—recommence their love-hate relationship, I was a happy and contented man once more. The next month we spent sailing slowly and happily through the islands of Greece towards the mainland and Athens. In all, we visited about 15 islands and were forced to the conclusion that we had arrived about ten years too late. Viewed from a few miles off, the mountainous, arid beauty of each island is breathtaking. The little whitewashed villages clinging precariously to the valley slopes, with the houses huddled higgledy-piggledy in tightly packed glorious confusion, pleases the eye much more than any planned design ever could. On closer inspection, however, much of the beauty is lost—in the tourist trampled villages, the local people have all become sour waiters or boutique owners—and the frequented beaches display a topsoil of discarded plastic, whilst the 'undiscovered beaches' are covered in oil. Add to this the fact that Greece is expensive, that the wind is either non-existent or blowing a gale force and it is hard to understand the islands' continued popularity among yachtsmen.

Happily for us, we found that the great majority of tourists and yachties, with their well-developed 'herding' instinct, spent most of their time in sardine-like togetherness at the 'known' spots, so we had many secluded anchorages completely to ourselves. One day in particular, alone in a beautiful little bay, we spent the evening sitting quietly on the tiny sandy beach watching all the wildlife arrive for their evening drink at the only waterhole on this small, uninhabited island— the name of which I am not prepared to divulge!

Of the well-known islands we visited perhaps the most interesting was Tinos. The main harbour town was far from inspiring for it has a supposedly miracle-working icon. It was with great horror that I watched all the superstitious pilgrims arriving by ferry to crawl on their hands and knees up the hill to the church in the vain hope of some miraculous cure for whatever ailed them—and being ripped off by the local stall holders who line the route.

Further along the coast, however, we were forced to anchor in a small bay by gale force winds. The vicious squalls blowing down the valley made life on board Shrimpy so uncomfortable that we decided to camp ashore for the duration of the storm. To get all the gear we would need on to the beach involved a lot of hard swimming because it was too windy to launch our little plastic dinghy, but eventually we had a snug little camp set up in the lee of a cliff and spent the next three days exploring the surrounding area.

It was soon obvious that in days gone by the whole of this dry rocky land had been intensely cultivated and highly populated. Tiny two-metre wide roads between high dry-stone walls meandered through terraced fields and small villages of very primitively built houses which were all deserted now and had been taken over by goats and donkeys. I could only gaze in awe at the work once expended to make this area habitable, all wasted, as it slowly crumbles back into the barren earth.

The nearest surviving village was three or four miles away, where the tarmac road to town ended and here we found the beauty of both town and people that long ago must have been so common throughout the islands. In a small cafe in this little village, well off the tourist track, chatting to the locals (mainly in sign language) letting the deliciously greasy, un-'MacDonaldised' Greek food slowly ooze into us, washed down with cool retsina wine, we managed to capture a small but precious part of days gone by.

The Greek isles are so close together that we had never been out of sight of land while sailing through them and, from Kea—the last island we visited—we could already see the mainland and a day's sail saw us arriving at one of the large, crammed full, yacht marinas which front the city of Athens. We had picked out this marina for a very good reason—we had been told that it was not yet completed and, therefore, had not got round to charging yachts mooring fees and were happy to find this was still the case when we arrived.

Just as we were entering the harbour, the motor packed up so, rather than put up the sails, I grabbed the tiller and started swinging it to and fro—for in this fashion I can usually scull Shrimpy through the water at about half a knot. Not this time, however, there was a sharp crack and the tiller came away in my hands—the wood had rotted through. After a lot of swearing plus some very unseamanlike manoeuvres, Iris and I managed to get Shrimpy tied up alongside.

Within an hour Iris had found an old bit of timber on the shore and I had shaped it, fitted it and its sparkling coat of varnish was drying in the sun. An example of one of Shrimpy's great advantages over her large sisters: almost any repair can be carried out simply, cheaply and with very little skill.

We were very unimpressed with the city of Athens and stayed only long enough to fill up with water and stores. After a fine day's sail, we reached the entrance to the Corinthian Canal, the combination of light winds, strong currents and a motor that refused to work, gave us some hectic moments before we managed to get alongside the dock.

I was pleased to find that unlike its big brothers—Panama and Suez— the Corinthian Canal has a minimum of regulations and paperwork— but, unfortunately, it more than makes up for this with a very stiff fee.

By the time we were due to transit, I still hadn't got the motor working, so an obliging powerboat threw us a line and towed us through. The vertical, towering walls of the canal make an impressive sight and evidence of previous landslides kept my voice very soft all the way through. Iris and I had anticipated two or three days of nice calm sailing in the landlocked Gulf of Corinth but this was not to be, for immediately after leaving the canal we were hit by a large thunderstorm which lasted most of the day and gave Shrimpy her first taste of cold, hard rain for many years. I was very surprised to find that she was still quite rainproof after so long in hot, dry sunshine.

Ever since we left Symi island, I had been navigating with the aid of roadmaps, as the price of proper charts was way beyond our means. From these maps we had chosen the town of Delphi for our next mailing address because it was shown to stand at the head of a well-protected bay. We found the bay easily enough and anchored in calm waters amid a fleet of local rowing boats. Rowing the dinghy ashore, we strolled around until we found the local Post Office, but were very

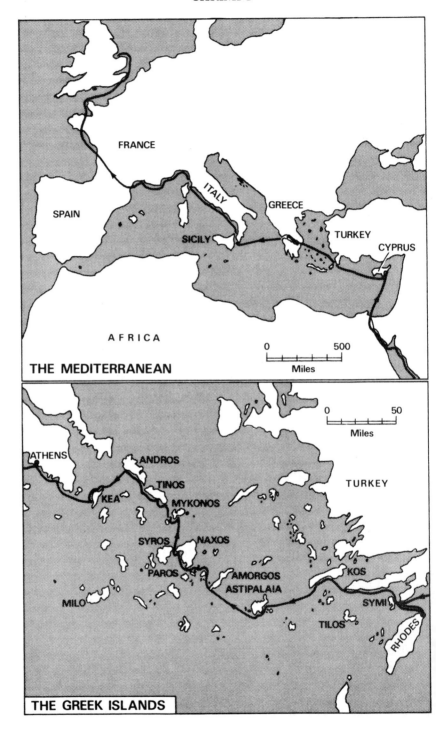

THE MEDITERRANEAN

THE GREEK ISLANDS

disappointed when told that there was not a single letter for us. Later that evening sitting in a cafe, I happened to tell a local what a beautiful little place Delphi was and, to my astonishment, he replied, 'I don't know, I've never been there'. Sure enough, further enquiries proved that our 'chart' was not too accurate and Delphi was actually an hour's bus ride away up in the mountains! The next day we had a beautiful ride into the countryside with a pile of mail waiting at the end of it.

After a difficult time sailing through the narrow mouth of the Gulf of Corinth, full of current and ferry boats, we arrived at the final and perhaps the prettiest Greek isle we were to visit—Ithaki. Much greener than the eastern islands, its snug port in a bay within a bay within a bay offered a perfectly protected anchorage. The little village, however, was a disappointment—poor quality food at higher than average prices, lack of friendliness and a fleet of charter yachts, all encouraged us to set sail after only a day.

In the short 250-mile sail across the Ionian sea from Ithaki to Cape Spartivento on the toe of Italy, the Mediterranean provided us with the full range of its crazy mixed-up weather; one day gale, one day calm and one day just perfect. Then, after a bumpy night spent anchored on the southernmost tip of Italy, we spent a day cruising slowly up the Straits of Messina to arrive in the port of Messina, Sicily. This dirty, oily harbour, its filthy water constantly churned by the 24-hour ferry service to Italy, made us feel really miserable, until a local tugboat of jovial Italians beckoned us alongside and soon the whole crew was involved in Iris's washing which was festooned around the tug's boiler-room for a rapid dry while we were bathed, fed and spent the evening watching the crew play a very involved card game. On this, as every other night, the losers of the game had to go off to buy dessert, which consisted of the sticky sweet cakes—dulces—so loved by Italians. The cakes rarely got eaten on this tug boat, however, as the crew had discovered long ago that they were marvellous weapons to attack winners of card games with!

175

21

The first and final winter
August 1 1979–June 28 1980

Leaving Sicily and struggling through the strong, dangerous currents of the Straits of Messina, we began to sail slowly northwards along the south western coast of Italy. Between Reggio di Calabria and Naples the coastline of Italy is extremely beautiful and we were happy to find that it was also very sparsely populated by yachts, mainly I suspect because of a complete lack of plug-in electrical points which most Mediterranean yachties need to survive. We managed to find an anchorage each night, which was just as well for I was really feeling the cold as winter was fast approaching—my first real winter since I left England over seven years ago. My thin blood, lulled to inactivity by the many years of warm tropical days, was having to work overtime and I could feel my bones shivering at even the thought of a swim!

By the time we had got as far north as the Tuscany coastline we noticed the clouds building up. The local radio station then warned us that the first autumn storm was fast approaching, so with all haste we sailed towards the famous little island of Elba, arriving in her snug, safe port just in time. A few days later, when the storm had abated and the sea was calm once more, we set off very early in the morning heading north towards Genoa. Iris was still asleep in the cabin while I sat outside giving Shrimpy's tiller an occasional nudge and watching the sun come up. As the light improved I saw that the sea ahead was covered by what appeared to be small boxes, curiously I altered course and sailed towards the nearest one. Minutes later, much to my astonishment, I fished out of the sea a carton of cigarettes! Pausing long enough to make sure my prize was real and the contents dry I began criss-crossing the sea in pursuit of all the other floating treasure and by the time Iris was rudely awoken by Shrimpy's erratic progress, her protestations were quickly calmed by the sight of the ten or so cartons I had already collected.

For the next hour we combined forces—Iris steering while I conned the boat from the bow until the horizon was boxless. We then counted our find—60 cartons (of three different makes), only half a dozen were spoiled and had to be thrown out. Cigarettes being the price they are in Europe this was treasure indeed! Leaving a contrail of cigarette smoke, we continued slowly along the coast of Italy and then France. The marina fees became prohibitive as we approached the Cote d'Azure, but luckily many of the marina bosses were willing to waive charges providing we only stayed overnight and got our tiny, tatty, wooden boat out of the harbour early in the morning, so that the rich owners of the huge plastic and stainless steel monstrosities wouldn't be offended by the sight of us.

Although disenchanted with the type of sailing the Mediterranean offers—bouncing along in fluky winds from one expensive crowded harbour to the next—we were happy to pull into the port of Baie des Anges, for here we met once again the yacht *Christophe* now resting after her circumnavigation and we had a wonderful reunion with Jean, Maryse, their child and the telegraph pole-sized tiki we had watched them buy in Tonga.

A few days further along the coast and Shrimpy was heading into the naval port of Toulon. Seeing French Naval vessels for the first time since Tahiti our thoughts drifted back to that Pacific island now many years behind us, and to Alain of the French Navy who had befriended us there and who had told us of his dreams of finding a girl, a boat and of sailing around the world. Only in the realms of fiction could it happen, but as we tied up to the jetty there stood Alain! What's more, next to him stood his bride and, to cap it all, a little further away sat the yacht which was ready to take them sailing off into the sunset! We spent the day with them in happy reunion. Later that evening as Iris and I strode slowly back to Shrimpy we were in for a further surprise.

A group of besuited businessmen were clustered on the jetty in front of our boat and as we neared them I was able to penetrate their civilised disguise to recognise the party of French scuba-divers I had met in the middle of the Red Sea. We were immediately whisked off to their club for yet another glorious reunion. During the course of the evening, Alain D'Orso—one of the members of the club—came up with a wonderful proposition: free moorings through the winter for Shrimpy at La Ciotat where he worked as chief surgeon of the hospital. He also offered us use of an apartment he owned there, overlooking the bay and volunteered to use his influence to help us find work in La Ciotat for the winter! Needless to say we happily accepted this amazing offer and, through the cold winter months, we passed the time in the warmth of central heating and the even greater warmth of the friendship of Alain and the many other people we met there.

Not having to live on Shrimpy, we were able to take plenty of time to give her a good clean out and repaint, so that by the time spring returned to the south of France and just before the annual influx of tourists arrived, we pointed a sparklingly bright Shrimpy out to sea on the final leg of her mammoth voyage. Giving a wide berth to the huge, noisy, crowded port of Marseilles, we headed towards the mouth of the River Rhône.

A mere 50 miles to go and we would enter the French canal system, but the Mediterranean wasn't going to let us off without a reminder of her power. A sudden squall and the jib ripped in half, then a quickly mounting wind soon had us running to a dubious anchorage in the lee of some tiny islands, where we had to sit for a whole day bobbing about in a sloppy sea trying as best we could to sew up the sail and getting as many stiches through our fingers as through the material.

When the blow had subsided we managed to reach Port Fos without further incident, but a different type of shock awaited us: the canal which by-passes the River Rhône between Fos and Arles was shut due to a collapsed bridge and the alternative route meant a 20 mile trip up the Rhône itself against the current of this mighty river which drains half of Europe.

Despite the fact that our little outboard motor, which had sat bravely and unprotestingly on Shrimpy's stern ever since Indonesia, was feeling very sick, we decided to give it a try. Luckily we found the river in one of her quieter moods and only had problems where she squeezes herself through the pretty little town of Arles. Just above Arles we turned off on to the Petit Rhône where the current is just as strong, but now we were going with it and quickly reached the Canal du Rhône à Sete. After locking through into the canal we were away from the currents and could sail leisurely along through the flat marshy delta lands of the Rhône called the Camargue, spending lazy hours watching the famous wild horses and bulls of the region, plus the amazing variety of birdlife. The most outstanding of the birds were the pink clouds of flamingoes that covered the shallow lakes alongside the canal, their feathers rustling in the strong Mistral winds.

Though still following the line of the coast, the canal eventually left the wild wastes of the Camargue behind. Its banks slowly began to sprout houses then whole villages, swing bridges swung, lifting bridges lifted and soon we entered the pretty little fishing port of Sete—a miniature Venice nestling between canal, lake and sea.

Here, in what we soon discovered was a very happy, friendly town, we prepared Shrimpy for her voyage across country to the Bay of Biscay, through the Canal du Midi and the Canal Lateral à la Garonne. A voyage of about 600 kilometres and 118 locks! We took her mast down, as the many bridges have only three metres clearance, and we almost buried her hull in a mass of old rubber tyres, to act as fenders and protect her from the rough walls of the many locks. Shrimpy then, for the first time, turned her back on the sea and set off inland. At an average speed of only 20 miles a day we climbed slowly, lock by lock, along this little used, beautiful canal, towards the summit. We met a number of yachts also using the canal as a short cut between the Atlantic and the Mediterranean. We also met a few working barges, but most of the sparse traffic consisted of large self-drive houseboats, hired out to tourists by two or three English firms situated along the canal. I would highly recommend this type of holiday for its relaxation and tranquil lifestyle—but not while my yacht is in the canal! For a small yacht like Shrimpy to share a lock with one of these houseboats and its inexperienced skipper is a hair-raising experience—more than once I thought I was going to lose my boat! Our load of rubber tyres really proved their worth because a few black marks on the hull are much better than a whole load of dents in it.

Despite the fact that parts of the canal are over 300 years old, we found that the whole trip was amazingly simple and the lock-keepers were very helpful and efficient—indeed we met one yacht which had made the journey from ocean to ocean in less than five days—although I cannot think why he wanted to go that fast. Each evening we would chug along until we found a perfect bit of canal-bank to tie up to, then we would light a fire and cook supper, while sipping one of the delicious local wines sold at deliciously low prices.

West of Toulouse the canal gets bigger and wider and loses much of its charm. Most of the locks are electrically and automatically operated. As you approach them you turn a stick suspended over the canal; the gates of the lock then open and you drive in. Two more tugs at another stick will empty (or fill) the lock and open the gates. All very modern and efficient but no quicker than the manually-operated locks and you have no smiling lock-keeper to pass the time of day with, as you help him open paddles and wind winches.

After reaching the summit of the canal and beginning to ease down towards the Atlantic Ocean, we found the locks less turbulent and our brushes with houseboats less alarming. Eventually we reached the huge estuary of the Gironde, put up the mast, got out the tide tables and set off to struggle northwards through the Bay of Biscay with its sudden squalls and notoriously bumpy seas. Despite the fact that June had now arrived and the full glory of summer was upon us, we found the Bay of Biscay appallingly cold. Each lump of spray which was blown into the cockpit set our teeth chattering and seemed to have no trouble at all finding its way through the heaps of pullovers, anoraks and oilskins which we now had to inhabit. For this reason we stayed very close to the coast, seeking the calm waters in the lee of off-lying islands, to help with this endeavour Shrimpy's small size, shallow draught and fast course-changing ability, once more came into their own and we sailed where many larger yachts could not hope to go.

Eventually we reached the mouth of the River Villaine and once more were able to turn inland, this time up river to Rennes, then by canal to

St Malo. Down came the mast again, out went all the tyres and off chugged the outboard. Less than half as long as the Canal du Midi, the Rennes canal is more than twice as beautiful as it meanders through the hills and woodlands of Brittany. With fewer houseboats to contend with and virtually no working barges, life was very easy indeed, even the local reporter who ran along the canal from lock to lock to get our 'story' could not spoil the beauty.

Around the end of June we found the air filled once again with the sharp unmistakable tang of the sea. The last lock emptied, the last lock-gate opened and there in front of us in all its foggy glory we could see the English Channel—home waters again!

22

The return
June 28–August 7 1980

'Sailing in the English Channel is like standing under a cold shower on an enormous lump of jelly tearing up £1 notes'—eight years ago I thought that old saying was a joke. I used to laugh in company with all the other blobs of sodden, cold, oilskinned sailors at the landlubbers who couldn't understand the 'fun', the 'challenge' the 'exhilaration' of bashing up and down the Channel in a small yacht. I don't laugh about it any more, the cold shower has turned to ice and the £1 notes have become £10 and the only reason I am continuing to sail up the Channel is because it's the only way to get home. It's amazing how the lazy warm tropical seas can change the outlook of all but the toughest masochists!

From St Malo we sailed to Jersey, where Iris had her first encounter with all the stodgy English food that she loves to hate, but the doughy bread and overcooked vegetables, while bringing on indigestion, also brought back fond memories of the many English friends we had met sailing on yachts throughout the world. One of these friends was Mr 'Happy Days' George himself—a guy so in love with life that it is almost obscene. We had met him in Bali, we had met him in the Mediterranean and now here he was in Jersey. His smiling face did more to warm us than any English sunshine could as he showed us round the town and chatted about old times.

As we sailed through the Channel Islands—Jersey—Sark—Alderney— the weather was far from kind so, as usual, I got the dinghy out at each anchorage and went on a tour of the other yachts—hoping to pass the rainy days swapping books, charts and gossip but, sadly, I discovered that most of the weekend Channel-hopping yachties are a totally different breed—much too busy playing at roughy-toughy sailors to even have non-nautical books on board; all they seem to want to talk about is boats and new gadgets for boats.

Leaving the Channel Islands we sailed slowly along the French coast stopping overnight in various expensive marinas, not from choice, but because there is virtually no anchorage left along the entire coastline that hasn't been turned into an expensive marina. Even where we found a pretty little port—such as Barfleur, which dries out completely at low tide and has nothing in the way of facilities—the price was just as high.

When we reached Calais it was time to turn north. Under full sail and motor we flew as fast as possible across the busy shipping lanes of the Channel and suddenly through the haze I had my first glimpse of England for eight years, Iris had her first glimpse ever. From Shrimpy's bilge I dug out the first chart I had ever used and looked at my outward course which I had laboriously marked thereon so many years ago. Comparing the outward position to our present one—which I keep in my head, not having felt the need to put pencil to chart for the past two or three years—we sailed on and, one mile south-east of the South Goodwin light vessel, Shrimpy crossed the outward line—completing the circumnavigation and becoming the smallest yacht ever to sail around the world! Out came the last bottle of French wine and we gave Shrimpy as much of it as we had ourselves—it seemed only fair.

We pulled in at Ramsgate to clear customs, who seemed more interested in whether or not I had paid VAT on the boat before I had left England, rather than whether or not we had actually sailed around the world.

One night at Ramsgate harbour prices was enough and next morning saw us sailing across the Thames estuary to Walton-on-the-Naze. My father and his new wife, Doris, drove down from Cambridge for a quiet reunion and arranged to meet us again further along the coast, they also told us that Cambridge was preparing quite a welcome for us. Continuing northwards along the coast Shrimpy seemed impatient to get home. After a brief stop at 'Wells'—the first port on my outward route—we entered the Wash. Trying an unmarked short-cut across the sandbanks we promptly ran aground and had to sit out a whole tide, but soon we were off again racing towards the River Ouse on a three knot flood.

In the fast fading evening light we entered the river and sailed through the town of King's Lynn. I had decided to keep going up river as long as the current was with us, it was quite dark but I knew this river well, or so I thought: turning a bend I saw to my horror a new low bridge spanning the river and we were charging towards it with our mast still up. Just in time we spotted a mooring buoy and managed to fight our way far enough back down river against the strong current to reach it and save the voyage from an ignominious end.

Next morning, with the mast dismantled for the final time, Shrimpy motored up river and through the first lock at Denver to moor in the non-tidal calm waters of the Ouse. The lock-keeper had been told to keep an eye out for us, as we were to be granted free passage up river to Cambridge, but I think he was also told to tip off the Press and TV because poor Shrimpy was soon swarming with them! We rested at Denver for two or three days giving ourselves and Shrimpy a final clean up with the generous aid of the local yacht club. My father, Doris and my sister, Debbie, with her two year old son Marc—who thankfully decided to call me Shane instead of uncle—arrived with a large picnic hamper full of carefully chosen stodge-free goodies in deference to Iris, and spent the day with us as close to Shrimpy as they could get without feeling seasick.

Chris South from the *Cambridge Evening News*, the local paper which had followed the whole voyage, arrived with a printed timetable projecting our progress up river, which I agreed to stick to after he had very diplomatically explained that the many people who wished to welcome us home would need to know exactly when we were going to arrive. At the appointed time we set off on the very last leg of the voyage. Eight years ago almost to the day Shrimpy had slipped quietly away from Cambridge down this very same river, but things were different now—the banks lined with people shouting welcome, throwing flowers to Iris, the Cambridge Sailing and Motorboat Clubs providing noisy escort, TV cameras whirring and the swans and ducks thinking of moving house, as Shrimpy slid back to the very same mooring she had left so long ago. We stepped ashore, the Mayor was there to greet us, a guard of honour by the sea cadets, the champagne flowing—spilling over the new turf—specially laid by Barclays Bank who now own the mooring, reunion with Janys, my other sister—whose children will also, hopefully, refuse to call me uncle—presentations, handshakes, a telegram from Nobby Clark who built Shrimpy, a telegram from Prince Philip wishing Shrimpy honourable retirement— 'in a swimming pool of course'.

Yes—home is the sailor, home from the sea. But we won't be staying long.

Appendices

A Technical details

Name of yacht: Super Shrimp. *Reg:* London 358661. *Design:* Sloop, Caprice Mk1. *Sail no:* C.159. *Designer:* Robert Tucker. *Builder:* C.E. Clark (at Cowes 1962). *Reg tonnage:* 2.10. *Length:* 18 ft 4 in. *Breadth:* 6 ft 2 in. *Draught:* 1 ft 8 in. *Construction:* Plywood. *Ballast:* 250 lb in each keel. *Sails:* 1 main, 1 jib, 1 Genoa, 1 running sail. *Provisions capacity:* 120 man-days. *Emergency equipment:* Flares (red, orange, white); plastic 2-man dinghy and paddles.

B The voyage in figures

Length of voyage: 30,000 miles approx. *Duration:* 8 years. *Cost of navigational gear, etc:* £50. *Amount of previous sailing knowledge:* Nil. *Funds available for voyage:* £30. *Long legs:* The Atlantic (Canaries—Barbados) 40 days; the Pacific (Galapagos—Marquesas) 45 days; the Indian Ocean (Malaysia—Sri Lanka) 10 days; the Indian Ocean (India—French Somaliland) 28 days. *Pleasure gained:* Incalculable.

C Navigational equipment

Compass: 1 Davies plastic, 1 ex-army prismatic (hand bearing). *Radio:* Vega Sebna receiver 8-band (Russian). *Watch:* Rolex 'Submariner'. *Sextant:* Ebbco plastic. *Charts:* Various (continually swapped with yachts heading in the opposite direction). *Books and tables: Nautical Almanac* (new one every 2nd year). *Burton's tables. Little Ship Celestial Navigation,* Rantzen. Highly recommended. *Reed's Almanac* (1972 and 1980 only). *Extras:* 2 pencils, 1 parallel ruler. And that's all!